Canadian Biography Series

DAVID CRONENBERG: A DELICATE BALANCE

Ready for the launch of
Naked Lunch *in* 1992.

David Cronenberg

A DELICATE BALANCE

Peter Morris

ECW PRESS

CANADIAN CATALOGUING IN PUBLICATION DATA

Morris, Peter, 1937–
David Cronenberg : a delicate balance
Includes bibliographical references.
ISBN 1-55022-191-4

1. Cronenberg, David. 2. Motion picture producers
and directors – Canada – Biography. I. Title.

PN1998.3.C76M67 1993   791.43′ 0233′ 092   C94-930009-8

This book has been published with the assistance of the Ministry
of Culture, Tourism and Recreation of the Province of Ontario, through
funds provided by the Ontario Publishing Centre, and with the assistance
of grants from the Department of Communications, The Canada
Council, the Ontario Arts Council, and the Government of Canada
through the Canadian Studies and Special Projects Directorate of the
Department of the Secretary of State of Canada.

Design and imaging by ECW Type & Art, Oakville, Ontario.
Printed by Imprimerie Gagné, Louiseville, Québec.

Distributed by General Distribution Services,
30 Lesmill Road, Toronto, Ontario M3B 2T6,
(416) 445-3333, (800) 387-0172 (Canada), FAX (416) 445-5967.
Distributed to the trade in the United States exclusively
by InBook, 140 Commerce Street, P.O. Box 120261,
East Haven, Connecticut, U.S.A. 06512,
(203) 467-4257, FAX (203) 469-8364.
Customer service: (800) 243-0138, FAX (800) 334-3892.

Published by ECW PRESS,
2120 Queen Street East, Toronto, Ontario, Canada M4E 1E2.

ACKNOWLEDGEMENTS

I am indebted to the many critics and journalists who have interviewed David Cronenberg and written about his work since the late sixties. My special thanks go to Chris Rodley, and to William Beard and Piers Handling, who have conducted extensive interviews with him. I am also grateful for the contributions of my researcher, James Luscombe. My thanks to Sandra Tucker of David Cronenberg Productions for checking the manuscript for errors and for her assistance in obtaining permissions to reproduce the photographs. I should also like to thank Dallas Harrison for his thoughtful and careful editing of the manuscript. The responsibility for errors of fact or opinion is, of course, mine.

Illustrations are from the collections of the National Archives in Ottawa, the Cinematheque Ontario in Toronto, the British Film Institute in London, the *Globe and Mail*, and the *Toronto Star* and are reproduced by permission of the copyright owners.

As always, I owe much to my wife, Louise Dompierre, for her love, support, and critical encouragement.

This book is dedicated to the late Jay Scott, critic extraordinaire, who brought his passionate eye and sharp critical insight to bear on the films of David Cronenberg. If he had liked this book, it would have been praise enough.

— Peter Morris
September 1993

The author and publisher gratefully acknowledge the use of the photos that appear in this book. They are published courtesy of the following: cover photo, source the Stills Collection, Moving Image and Sound Archives, Ottawa; frontispiece illustration, Tibor Kelley, © the *Globe and Mail*, is used by permission of the *Globe and Mail*, Toronto; illustration 2, © Peter Morris, is used by permission of Peter Morris; illustration 3, © Peter Morris, is used by permission of Peter Morris; illustration 4, source Cinematheque Ontario, © David Cronenberg, is used by permission of David Cronenberg; illustration 5, source Cinematheque Ontario, © David Cronenberg, is used by permission of David Cronenberg; illustration 6, source Cinematheque Ontario, © David Cronenberg, is used by permission of David Cronenberg; illustration 7, source Cinematheque Ontario; illustration 8, source Cinematheque Ontario; illustration 9, source Cinematheque Ontario; illustration 10, source the Stills Collection, Moving Image and Sound Archives, Ottawa; illustration 11, M. Slaughter, © the *Toronto Star*, is used by permission of the *Toronto Star*; illustration 12, source the Stills Collection, Moving Image and Sound Archives, Ottawa; illustration 13, source the British Film Institute, Stills, Posters, and Designs; illustration 14, Jack Dobson, © the *Globe and Mail*, is used by permission of the *Globe and Mail*, Toronto; illustration 15, source the British Film Institute, Stills, Posters, and Designs; illustration 16, source Cinematheque Ontario; illustration 17, Barrie Davis, © the *Globe and Mail*, is used by permission of the *Globe and Mail*, Toronto; illustration 18, source the Stills Collection, Moving Image and Sound Archives, Ottawa; illustration 19, source Cinematheque Ontario; illustration 20, J. Mahler, © the *Toronto Star*, is used by permission of the *Toronto Star*; illustration 21, source Cinematheque Ontario.

TABLE OF CONTENTS

LIST OF ILLUSTRATIONS

David Cronenberg

A DELICATE BALANCE

A SIMPLE LIFE, A COMPLEX ART

In the seventies, David Cronenberg was dubbed Canada's own "Baron of Blood," "Prince of Horror," and "Schlockmeister." He was regularly attacked by custodians of good taste as a vulgarian whose sole aim was to titillate mass audiences with increasingly outrageous shock effects. Such critics agonized over the contrast between the purity of his early avant-garde features and the depravity they found in his commercial features. Other critics pointed to recurrent themes informing his films — in contrast to the work of other visceral horror directors such as, say, John Carpenter. Cronenberg's images, it was said, might be shocking, perverse, even disgusting, but they revealed a fascination with the myriad ways that we can be betrayed by our minds and bodies. His films were not the traditional horror of ghoulies, ghosts, aliens, or rampaging robots but powerful images of "the horror within." His film worlds reflected the shifting interfaces of mind and body, the rational and irrational, the conscious and subconscious. They explored our often problematic relationship with science and technology. They implied that, if evolutionary theory were correct, then there was no reason to believe that humanity as we know it would be the end of the road.

I well remember my first viewing of *Shivers*. I had already seen *Stereo* and *Crimes of the Future* several times and greatly admired them. In the early seventies, Cronenberg had told me that he was hoping to make a commercial horror film. If I had found this puzzling, then I had no doubt ascribed it, somewhat simplistically, to the filmmaker's need to earn a living. Hoping for the best, but predictably fearing the worst, I went to see *Shivers* (then titled, more appositely, *The Parasite Murders*) at an Ottawa movie theatre noted for its screening of exploitation movies. I was astonished by the film's raw energy, its bold inventiveness and striking imagery. Added to these were the same intelligence, wit, and quirky sense of humour that had marked the earlier films. Of course, some of the dialogue in *Shivers* was unconvincing and the acting often weak. But this was a horror film like none that had preceded it. There could be no doubt that this was a film by a director with his own vision.

By the nineties, his films had won numerous film festival awards, he had received an unprecedented three Genie Awards as Best Director, and he had been honoured at major retrospectives of his work in London, Paris, Toronto, Tokyo, Montreal, and other cities. He had metamorphosed, in critical opinion at least, from a reviled director of (albeit successful) schlock films to a widely honoured director of international stature. Throughout, he had remained almost dogmatically loyal to his artistic vision, which, among other things, insisted that there was no difference between high art and popular culture. And, perhaps most remarkably, he had done so while operating within the commercial film industry — that well-known minefield of artistic integrity.

Many of the early interviews with Cronenberg note, almost with a sense of bewilderment, the contrast between his gruesome films and his bespectacled, composed appearance and diffident, even scholarly, manner. This bewilderment is curious because it assumes that there is a mirror-image relationship between the moral characters of artists and their work: an assumption that the creators of violent and grotesque images must themselves be violent and grotesque. This rather simplistic linking of artwork with character has continued to haunt Cronenberg, with some critics assuming that he endorses whatever he depicts. Although he has defended himself many times on this issue, perhaps he put it most plainly more than a decade ago. "It's a paradox," he said to Sandra Peredo in 1981. "The difference between what your art does and what your life is." This statement also reflects another characteristic of his work: a tendency to understand simultaneously all sides of a story and to see apparently contradictory elements as part of the same thing. He has spoken of the contrast some people assume between his "warm, friendly" persona and his "grotesque, disgusting" films as real for them. But, as he told Chris Rodley, "For me, those two parts of myself are inextricably bound together." He has often spoken of this as a sense of balance, something that might be thought of as a curse, but (as he remarked to William Beard and Piers Handling) "maybe it's very Canadian, too." Critics, according to their tastes, have considered this characteristic as either the virtue of ambiguity or the vice of ambivalence.

This balance aside, common sense tells us that every work of art bears the stamp of its creator. Recent psychoanalytical approaches to criticism have offered a deepened understanding of the interaction between artists and their work. For such critics, artistic products are less an *expression* of the unconscious than a resolution and sublimation of repressions; the work is *part* of the artist's life, not the converse. As Julia Kristeva has argued, the work of art might well be the site of an artist's conquered melancholia. It is, then, conceivable that a bold and aggressive artist might well be modest and retiring in private life.

With this in mind, it is perhaps not surprising to learn that Cronenberg grew up in a middle-class home with a supportive family environment. His university experiences in the sixties were no different in their rejection of establishment values than those of thousands of others. His first filmmaking was as one of many student "underground" filmmakers. In many ways, he is an ordinary Canadian of his generation. Only with his transition to commercial production and the visceral horror of *Shivers* can he be said to have sharply differentiated himself from his peers. It was this transition that also led to his facing virulent critical abuse. In part this was because some perceived that he had "sold out," compromising his artistic integrity for box-office success. While this biography will examine Cronenberg's transition to commercial production, it is fair to say that, though he has made concessions, they were infinitesimally small compared with other commercial directors. In fact, he has remained remarkably faithful not only to his own vision but also to working with his own production team and according to his own production methods — including shooting in Canada, not the States.

Another element of the critical abuse that Cronenberg initially faced was rooted in a widely held assumption that the horror genre was inherently incapable of containing personal visions. While Cronenberg has proved that assumption wrong, it is, at least in part, because he redefined the genre to his own specifications. When *Shivers* was released, he told Robert Martin that he had no desire to become Canada's Roger Corman. "I'll be the first Cronenberg," he said. "I've always been very ambitious that way." Cronenberg's sense of himself as an artist will form a central theme of this biography.

Cronenberg has had a remarkable first quarter-century in filmmaking. He stubbornly persisted in butting his head against the dominant naturalist aesthetic of Canadian cinema. He insisted on projecting his own vision, one inspired more by surrealism than realism. And he survived to triumph over his earlier, and even later, detractors.

Developments in Cronenberg's career have often paralleled changes in Canadian film itself. In some measure, his story is also the story of thirty years of Canadian cinema. He has always been positioned to take advantage of different situations: from the independent, underground cinema of the sixties to the industrialization of Canadian film in the seventies under the aegis of the Canadian Film Development Corporation and favourable tax laws and, finally, a return to a preference for quality over profits in the eighties. He is now secure ("a bankable director" as the industry calls it) and has the freedom to choose that for which he once had to fight. In this context, his success as a nonnaturalistic filmmaker has also helped to open the door for a new generation of Canadian filmmakers, including Atom Egoyan, Patricia Rozema, and Guy Maddin, who also work outside realist modes.

And, far from least, David Cronenberg has given us many pleasures.

AN ELUSIVE INDIVIDUALITY

We may our ends by our beginnings know.

— *Sir John Denham*

David P. Cronenberg was born on 15 March 1943 in Toronto, Ontario. His parents, Milton and Esther (née Sumberg), already had a daughter, Denise. They lived at 446 Crawford Street near College Street in west Toronto, an area that is now labelled by the city as "Little Italy." It was then, and is now, an immigrant transition area — a district to which newcomers gravitate for support. It had once been predominantly Jewish, but, when Cronenberg was growing up, the Jews were already beginning to move out to more affluent suburbs and being replaced by Italians, Irish Catholics, and a smattering of Middle Eastern peoples. The Cronenbergs were to join this exodus in 1958 when they moved to 66 Hillhurst Boulevard in a recently developed residential area north of Eglinton Avenue.

Despite the waves of postwar immigration that would soon radically transform the city's character, Toronto in the fifties was a respectably ordinary and rather unexciting place. It was not that different from the city British poet Rupert Brooke described some forty years earlier. "Toronto," he wrote in a letter,

... has an individuality, but an elusive one; yet not through any queerness or difficult shade of eccentricity; a subtly normal and indefinably obvious personality. It is a healthy,

13

cheerful city; a clean-shaven, pink-faced, respectably dressed, fairly energetic, unintellectual, passably sociable, well-to-do, public school-and-varsity sort of city.

It was also a city, we should remember, that continued to attempt the censorship of artworks through the midsixties, a city from which many artists then preferred to escape. Cronenberg himself told William Beard and Piers Handling that the Toronto in which he grew up

had a certain kind of stifling order. This was the Eisenhower era, which masked something very delicious, which turned out to be partially chaos but also turned out to be partially just raw energy. There was a lot of sexual energy being repressed by society then, but also artistic and creative energy, not in my own household, but in school and society.

Artistic energies were by no means "repressed" in the Cronenberg home. The parents actively encouraged their children's creative imaginations, whether in popular culture or high art. Milton was a freelance writer who had run a bookstore (The Professor's Bookshop) during the Depression. He wrote early Canadian comic books, wrote and edited the magazine *True Canadian Stories*, and wrote the stamp-collecting column for the *Toronto Telegram* for some twenty-five years. He was "a rabid bibliophile," Cronenberg told interviewer Chris Rodley. Esther was an accompanist for choirs and a rehearsal pianist for the National Ballet of Canada. David's sister, Denise, recollected the home environment for John Colapinto: "We used to fall asleep to the sound of my father's typewriter. Then we'd wake to my mother's string quartets." Denise became a dancer with the National Ballet and eventually joined her brother's production team as chief costumer.

David Cronenberg remembers rooms engulfed by books. "There were walls made of books, literally; they were piled so high there were corridors made of books, thousands of them," he told Beard and Handling. He also recalls being surprised when he visited his friends' homes and discovered walls without books. It was, in short, a home environment totally supportive and accepting of the arts, of writing and creativity. In many ways, it was a relatively contented, even placid, childhood for Cronenberg. Certainly it was one far removed from the kind of traumatic, formative family experiences often cited in the backgrounds of artists. There was not even a troubling religious experience to reject because both his parents had abandoned the Jewish religion many years before — while encouraging him to form his own opinions about it. The most terrible thing that he can recall happening to him was at eighteen, when his favourite cat died of cancer and pneumonia. He recalled the event to Katherine Govier: "One day she had these bumps. They were a bit like the bumps people get in *Shivers*, now that I think of it. . . ." Despite the happy home environment, Cronenberg's cousin, the artist Claire Weissmann, told Mark Czarnecki that she remembers him as being afflicted by a "great sense of death."

Cronenberg was educated at Dewson Street Public School, a few blocks from his home, then at Kent Senior School on Dufferin Street and at Harbord Collegiate Institute. Later, when the family moved, he attended North Toronto Collegiate Institute. Many of the students there were from the affluent neighbourhood of Forest Hill, and it was there that he met many of the people who would later become part of his personal and professional life. Not the least momentous of the friendships he formed was with Stephen Zeifman from Forest Hill, whose sister, Carolyn, would become Cronenberg's second wife.

Like most young people, he formed passionate — and sometimes passing — interests. Whether he wanted to become a veterinarian or a classical guitarist (he studied guitar for eleven years) or a lepidopterist, his parents encouraged his enthusiasms and did not complain when they waned. (One adolescent interest that has continued is his passion for racing motorbikes and cars.) He surmises now, from his position as a parent, that their technique was simply a natural one for them. As he told Rodley,

I think what I got at home was an unshakeable, totally realistic faith in my own abilities, and a confidence in being able to do what I wanted to do. We communicated a lot, and very well. I was never frustrated because I couldn't talk to my parents, or any of those things that are common conflicts. . . . I think of myself as being resolutely middle class, and yet when I see what true middle-class values are, they're not mine. My parents really invented their own version of what it is to be middle class.

However, his teenage years in a more affluent neighbourhood gave him a special sense of a kind of middle-class normalcy different than that of his own home. As he later told Govier, "Those houses in Forest Hill are filled with crazy people, all going through the most bloodcurdling things." The pathology of bourgeois life became one of the central metaphors in his work.

Not all members of Cronenberg's family approved of Milton and Esther's parental approach; some aunts and uncles felt that David was being pampered to the point of adversely affecting his character. Claire Weissmann remembers the criticisms. "The judgments made," she told Colapinto, "were that he . . . was being spoiled and indulged, and that we should all learn a routine and be disciplined. Whereas," she continued, "in fact, he's succeeded precisely because of the kind of home he had — which is not unusual [now] but sure as heck was in the 1950s."

Throughout Cronenberg's high-school years, two key interests emerged: fiction and science. To his mind, these interests were not incompatible because he had not learned, he told Beard and Handling, that he "was supposed to be schizophrenic about it." This mingling of interests is an early example of his developing sense of balancing apparent incongruities. An initial interest in nature and animals (including insects) developed into an engagement with biology, biochemistry, and what he described to Rodley as "the physical basis of human thought and imagination." Cronenberg also indicated that he based the young boys in the prologue of *Dead Ringers* partly on himself. "I did wear glasses as a kid, I was interested in science and I was precocious. I'm still ambivalent about it all, because I loved it. . . . So in a way I completely identify with those two little monsters."

Cronenberg's reading was voracious and eclectic: comic books, fantasy and science fiction, the "underground" novels of the Beats, the French symbolists, and the work of symbolist-influenced writers such as James Joyce and William Butler Yeats. The novels of William S. Burroughs and Vladimir Nabokov were later to become lasting influences.

Cronenberg was also an insatiable, if uncritical, patron of movies at neighbourhood theatres, the College Moviehouse and the Pylon. For him, the weekly (and even biweekly) movie was like any other object of popular culture that he absorbed. It was not until his university years that he became aware of film's potential to create fictional universes as powerful as those in literature — though he has never thought of himself as a cinephile. Even today, he maintains no more than a lively, intelligent interest in other people's films, while his understanding of literature and literary criticism is prodigious. At the same time, one cannot watch numerous films without absorbing some sense of how different directors use such elements as staging — even if one might discount the direct influence of any particular film-maker.

Television came late to the Cronenberg household. Milton, the bibliophile, was very resistant to television, and Cronenberg remembers having to go to the houses of friends to watch *Howdy Doody*. When the set finally arrived, he became as gluttonous in devouring shows as he had been in watching movies and reading comic books.

There are several patterns that emerge from these early years. One, certainly, is that fiction and science were for Cronenberg equally creative, if parallel, worlds. Another is that he was prepared to absorb, like a sponge, almost anything that crossed his path and equally prepared, also like a sponge, to reject anything that was not useful in sustaining him. Yet another is that the

FIGURE 2

*The first Cronenberg family home, on Crawford
Street in Toronto (recent photograph).*

young Cronenberg's venues for absorption were essentially solitary ones: reading, watching movies and television, observing events in the natural world or under a microscope, and, later, writing. In high school, he avoided team sports and social events, preferring to spend time by himself or with one or two others. The description he wrote of himself for the Harbord Collegiate *Review* reflects this: "David is a writer and a perceptive genius as well. As such, he is an observer. These, being his own terms, are thus indisputable. This is how he explains the fact that he has done nothing during his five years at Harbord. He merely observes." We might find his solitariness strange, given his supportive family environment, until we remember that his parents were both artists and that art is essentially a solitary activity despite its necessary links to the daily world: a rehearsal to attend, a deadline to meet.

There is, though, another aspect of Cronenberg's developing introspective personality that we should note. Solitariness is inevitably associated with feeling somewhat disassociated from, or outside of, one's particular social group. Cronenberg has agreed that he felt something of an outsider during his adolescence. (This sense need not be a traumatic or even troubling experience, especially when it is chosen and not a role forced on the individual by the social group.) His feeling of being an outsider was undoubtedly reinforced during his years at both Harbord and North Toronto Collegiate Institutes. At that time, Jewish students comprised by far the largest proportion of the student body. Cronenberg recalled that it was there that he "learnt about Jewishness, not from my family. That's where I got to understand all the North American Jewish stereotypes, the overtly possessive, suffocating Jewish mother. All that kind of stuff." As he told Rodley, he continues to "feel mildly but definitely like an outsider in any Jewish function or celebration," even though he also continues to identify himself as Jewish. At the same time, he always thought that "I would much more likely be put in jail for my art than for my Jewishness," as he put it to Beard and Handling.

This tenuous outsider status persisted during Cronenberg's university years and after: the aspiring artist adrift in the science faculty; the prize-winning writer switching to the unknown field of filmmaking; the internationally recognized avant-garde filmmaker attempting to break into the mainstream film industry. It is almost as if, in his early years at least, acceptance in one field encouraged him to move to another in which he had outsider status. As he later said to Beard and Handling, ". . . I suppose underneath I always have a feeling that my existence as a member in standing of the community is in grave jeopardy for whatever reason."

This sense is particularly relevant given that one of the most consistent traits of Cronenberg's films is their depiction of outsider characters in central roles. Although these outsiders vary considerably from film to film, most often they are eccentric characters who do not fit into their social group, often by choice but occasionally not. Sometimes they are involved in science or technology, and almost always they are loners. The character of Bill Lee in *Naked Lunch* is only the most recent example of this trait in Cronenberg's films.

CHOICES, CHOICES . . .

Cronenberg's passion for reading soon developed into the practice of writing. And, given his fascination with the workings of the natural world, it is perhaps not surprising that he sometimes contemplated blending his two interests in the manner of writers such as Isaac Asimov. He says that he cannot remember a time when he didn't want to write and has a clear memory of writing a "novel" at ten — a novel that was barely two pages long! By his midteens he was writing short stories, following the advice of the various magazines that offered counsel to aspiring and professional writers. (He would later follow a similar path when

FIGURE 3

*The second Cronenberg family home, on Hillhurst
Boulevard in Toronto (recent photograph).*

he had to learn about filmmaking.) When he was sixteen, he submitted one of his stories to the *Magazine of Fantasy and Science Fiction*. Although it was rejected, he received a letter from the editors encouraging him to submit others. As it turned out, he largely abandoned short-story writing until his university years. His commitment to the biological sciences was intensifying, and his reading interests were increasingly turning in the direction of experimental fiction.

Interestingly, his parallel passion for the *images* of popular culture in movies and television elicited no matching response in a desire to create them. In the context of the times, though, this was hardly surprising. In the late fifties and early sixties, virtually all movies and much of television came from elsewhere, mostly Hollywood. Cronenberg himself does not recall seeing a Canadian film before the midsixties and has only vague memories of Canadian TV drama. (He must certainly have seen National Film Board documentaries in high school, but he probably did not consider them real films.) However, though he could scarcely have been aware of them, there had been attempts to establish feature-film production in Toronto while he was in high school. Six feature films were made in Toronto between 1958 and 1961. Two were written and directed by a twenty-four-year-old television writer, Sidney Furie. Both *A Dangerous Age* and *A Cool Sound from Hell* dealt with young people rebelling against the system. Both were well received by critics abroad, who hailed Furie as a promising young director. However, both were ignored by Canadian critics and received almost no release in Canada until some years later when they played at drive-ins and on television. Not surprisingly, Furie left the country (as many others had done before him) to work in Britain and Hollywood.

Two other features were made by the writer-director team of William Davidson and Norman Klenman. At least one of them (*Now That April's Here*) would have interested the young Cronenberg, had he known of it, as it was based on four short stories by Morley Callaghan. However, despite its qualities, it ran for only one week in Toronto and was not seen again for many years. The second film, *Ivy League Killers*, remained unreleased for five years. The other two features of the time were both consciously designed for commercial release. Even if Cronenberg had seen Julian Roffman's *The Bloody Brood* and *The Mask*, they would likely not have remained in his memory as Toronto-made films. Whether Cronenberg would have been forever discouraged from filmmaking had he known of these setbacks is, of course, impossible to know. For others, however, they formed one more step on the road to establishing a viable feature-film industry. Through the midsixties, film directors, producers, and others brought increasing pressure on governments to act in support of the industry. Eventually the federal government introduced new funding and other policies to promote the film industry. These policies were to become key elements in nurturing Cronenberg's later film career.

However, for the university-bound Cronenberg in 1963, the choice was not between film and literature; it was between science and literature. High school had finally taught him that they were not the same thing, despite his continuing belief, expressed to Rodley, that "the best scientists are as mad, creative and eccentric as writers and artists of any kind." He had had excellent English and science teachers at high school, and all had tried to encourage him to continue studies in their own disciplines. He eventually opted for science, sensibly concluding that one needed to be *taught* science but could not be taught to write through courses in English literature.

THE UNIVERSITY YEARS

In 1963 Cronenberg (an Ontario Scholar) enrolled as an honours science student at the University of Toronto. It took him only a few months to realize that he had made the wrong choice. While the subjects he studied continued to excite him, he felt suffocated by the ways that they were taught. "What I needed," he told Chris Rodley, "was a feeling of excitement, discovery, creativity; the infinite possibility that you get with the study of literature, and which you should get with the study of science." Instead, "the way science was presented at university then was very dry and alien to me . . . detached, distracted and passionless." Not surprisingly, yet again he felt himself "truly an outsider. I couldn't get in. . . . I didn't have any friends among my classmates. . . ." To William Beard and Piers Handling he recalled that "Spiritually, I did not last more than a couple of months. By the end of the year I was not going to classes. I was hanging out in the Junior Common Room of University College at the University of Toronto, talking to everybody in the arts." He dropped out of the science program soon after a short story of his won the prestigious Epstein Award. The following academic year he switched to honours English language and literature. In making the transfer, he was again fully supported by his parents who understood that he was still searching for a sense of direction. Now he felt at home among others who were as passionate and excited about the same books and writers as he was. He had a good academic year and was awarded the Gertrude Lawler Scholarship for finishing first at University College.

When he later turned to filmmaking, it became evident that his intense interest in science had not abated; in fact, it shaped his vision. Scientific themes dominated his work until recent years. And he has often remarked that the doctors and scientists in his films reflect his own persona. As he told John Colapinto in 1986, "I've always said I'm the scientist in all my movies. My movies are experiments, and the studio is my lab." However, of all the scientific influences that he encountered, one deserves special mention. This is the theory of Emergent Evolutionism. A variation on basic Darwinian evolutionary theory, it argues that evolution was not always a continuous, gradual process. Leaps could occur (and had been observed) in such a way that biological novelties emerged. Because these "emergent events" were genuinely novel they could not be predicted, only observed

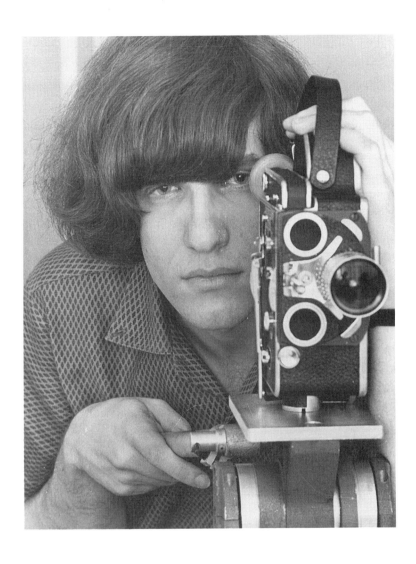

FIGURE 4

*The aspiring filmmaker poses for his first
promotional photograph in 1966.*

after the fact. Many biologists endorse the theory as offering a valid description of what happened at critical stages in terrestrial evolution — not least that of humans.

Emergent Evolutionism conditioned much of Cronenberg's early work. This is apparent in the name of his first production company, Emergent Films — a reference to the theory but also to his own "emerging" role. More significantly, it is apparent in the thematic core of his films, which are based on a series of "What if . . . ?" emergent events: What if telepaths? (*Stereo, Scanners*); What if a womanless world? (*Crimes of the Future*); What if a scientifically created parasite runs amok? (*Shivers*); What if human flesh begins to develop in unexpected ways? (*Rabid, The Brood, Videodrome*). Although the Emergent influence gradually became more diffuse in his work, it is still clearly present in the random genetic splicing in *The Fly* and the trifurcated womb in *Dead Ringers*.

"WORDS BEGET IMAGES"

Words beget images, and image is virus.

— *William S. Burroughs,* Naked Lunch

In 1964 Cronenberg was still convinced that he would become a novelist, and he gradually began to adopt a style befitting his ambition. His friend, the writer Norman Snider, told Colapinto that, when they first met, Cronenberg "was still the ex-science student, with short hair, glasses, the short-sleeved shirt with the pencil holder in the pocket." Photographs from a few years later show full and flowing hair brushing the top of a casual shirt or, in one shot at least, an Edwardian jacket and paisley shirt. He was to continue this fastidious sense of grooming, later claiming to Snider that to reach a state of inner perfection and equilibrium one's appearance must match. Certainly, in the sixties, he resembled an aesthete or dilettante more than he did the typical student rebel of the period. And that is probably how he saw himself. Although he was very much a part of his radical generation, he understood it more in artistic than in political terms. He had little interest in student protests and the political left. If pressed, he might well have agreed with William Burroughs, who argued in an interview that political change was pointless as it simply replaced one system with another. This apolitical stance returned to haunt Cronenberg in later years when some critics attacked him for failing to promote awareness of the potential for change through his characters. Cronenberg's invariable response has been to argue that inserting politics in a film turns it into propaganda. As he told Susan Ayscough in a hard-hitting interview on his political stance in 1983, "I think that art and propaganda are poles apart, and that they don't overlap." Ayscough described interviewing Cronenberg on politics as "a lot like playing hopscotch in a mine field."

Although Cronenberg stood somewhat aloof from the political changes of the sixties, he was inevitably a part of the radical transformations of the period. These were fuelled more by uncertainty than by any particular agenda, uncertainty that led to a questioning of virtually every established (and establishment) value. Politics, universities, schools, family life, all were questioned — as, indeed, were the arts and the tenets of "good taste." In literature, for example, young people "discovered" the work of modernist and experimental writers such as James Joyce, Vladimir Nabokov, William Burroughs, Henry Miller, T.S. Eliot, and others. The Beat movement was particularly influential because the Beats' creative work and lifestyles both vehemently rejected middle-class life and values and stressed a search for one's own consciousness. There was also renewed interest in those seen as precursors of the Beats or related to the work of writers such as Joyce and Nabokov. The symbolists and the surrealists, with their antinaturalistic emphasis on the significance of metaphor, allegory, and symbols, drew particular attention.

FIGURE 5

Shooting his second short film, From the Drain, *in 1966.*

On the evidence of the antinaturalistic tenor of his work, it is apparent that Cronenberg was greatly influenced by these writers — even if the influence is diffuse and not direct. It is evident most simply in the way that his images carry overtones not immediately relatable to plot and character, overtones that may well be set in opposition to others in later scenes. These elements, in part, give his films their pleasing sense of poetic ambiguity.

Two writers were particularly influential: Vladimir Nabokov and William Burroughs. In fact, Cronenberg admitted to Rodley that when he tried to write novels he was "possessed by Nabokov and Burroughs. One of the things I had trouble with as a writer was getting out of their clutches. I couldn't find my own voice." In retrospect, Burroughs seems to have been the most lasting influence. Cronenberg frequently quotes him in interviews, his films (especially the early ones) often reflect a Burroughs-like world, and, of course, he filmed *Naked Lunch* in 1991. This, the most famous of Burroughs's novels, was first published in the United States in 1962. (It had been published in Paris in 1959, and extracts had appeared in magazines such as the *Evergreen Review*.) It aroused a storm of controversy and at least one trial for obscenity. Three other novels were published in quick succession, forming a quartet whose formal experimentation (extending "cut-and-paste" collage techniques used by Gertrude Stein, John Dos Passos, and T.S. Eliot) was widely influential on a younger generation of writers. Equally influential in the context of the times were Burroughs's themes: a scathing scorn for both the middle class and the new totalitarian nation-states, their wars, corporate capitalists, and addictions; a concern for the mind-expanding potential of drugs as well as their effects of physical bondage and social victimization; and, not least, a pessimistic vision of a world trapped in parasitical, destructive sexuality and controlled by technological power groups. He was particularly interested in the realm of the irrational and the repressed. His personality and lifestyle were also intriguing: he had been a drug addict, dropped out of mainstream life, and lived as a classic bohemian artist in Central and South America and North Africa, spurned by the literary establishment. He became something of a legend to the youth culture of the sixties, among whom he was known as the "Beat Godfather" and the "Holy Monster." He made many sympathetic comments about youthful rebellion in interviews and in his work — though he was convinced that this rebellion was more cultural than political.

It would be surprising had the undergraduate Cronenberg not been attracted to such a radical artist and nonconformist. Burroughs, like Cronenberg, had had a relatively privileged bourgeois upbringing; and Cronenberg was to follow Burroughs in exploring the tensions and nightmares buried beneath the apparent placidity of bourgeois life. Almost everything Burroughs wrote Cronenberg seems to have read assiduously, and he must have been at least equally attracted to the writer's extreme personality and commitment to his art as to his radical writing styles. In later years Cronenberg would say that, while there were influences from Burroughs, he felt the connection was more one of parallel ideas. "One of the reasons you find a writer so compelling," he said to Rodley, "is that they crystallize for you stuff that's in you already. Images of addiction and body-consciousness, say." He recognized his own imagination and metaphors in Burroughs. "Not all of it. Not all of it in Burroughs, and not all of it in me. But so much of it, right there, stuff I could have written, except Burroughs had been doing it so much better and for so much longer." Certainly Burroughs could not have failed to recognize something of his own world in *Stereo* and *Shivers*, and there are Burroughs-like metaphors in all of Cronenberg's early films. Interestingly, Burroughs made several experimental films in 1965 with the English filmmaker Antony Balch (*Open Fire*; *Cut-Ups*; *Bill and Tony*), the same year that Cronenberg made his first film.

By 1965, film had become an essential ingredient in the counterculture of the period. While this prominence was sparked in part by the young filmmakers of the New Wave in France, it was also sparked because of film's perceived role outside establishment culture. Taking film seriously became one more option for young people to reject the tastes of their elders. It was only in his university years that Cronenberg began to consider film as something other than passive entertainment at the neighbourhood movie theatre. Like thousands of others of his generation, he saw the great European art films of the period — films by Federico Fellini, Ingmar Bergman, Alain Resnais, François Truffaut, Luis Buñuel, and others. With friends he attended screenings at the Toronto Film Society or in revue theatres such as The Little Cinema. Cronenberg has always insisted that none of the films he saw influenced him except in the sense that he understood it was possible for filmmakers to control their work just as novelists did. "[Y]ou entered a world of their own creation," he told Rodley, "when you went to see their films. That world was consistent from film to film. There was a tone, a feeling and dynamics that were consistently at work."

While young Europeans turned to the narrative feature-length film for their innovations, in North America the situation was different. Hollywood's control was then so absolute that it was virtually impossible for a newcomer to enter the industry. Young people quickly embraced a movement that had begun in New York and San Francisco. It insisted that the only valid use of the film medium was for self-expression. The filmmakers involved urged the creation of independent, personal, low-budget films that explored formal experimentation or expressed the author's obsessions, desires, or visions. Variously dubbed by its adherents as "New American Cinema," "The American New Wave," "The New York School," the term that finally caught on was "Underground Cinema" because of its rebellious connotations. *Playboy* magazine called them "far out films," using Beat slang. Some of the popular media adopted the term, as in the famous headline in the *Toronto Star*: "Thousands Flee Far-Out Film" — a reference to the 1964 screening at the University of Toronto of Michael Snow's *New York Eye and Ear Control*. Whatever they were called, the sexual obsessions (and often explicit sexual imagery) of many of the films made them a threat to guardians of public morality.

Even when not sexually explicit, many of these films used psychedelic or other nonnaturalistic imagery — an approach that many potential censors may have found even more threatening. (A classic example of this mind-set was the banning by British censors of the 1928 French film *Seashell and the Clergyman* with the comment: "It is so cryptic as to have no apparent meaning. If there is a meaning, it is doubtless objectionable.") Screenings of underground films were often harassed by police morality squads and obscenity charges. Toronto was by no means an exception, though the most amusing example was a nonevent. The Bohemian Embassy (a coffeehouse founded in 1960 as a meeting place for artists) began regular screenings of American underground films in the fall of 1965. These were to include Jack Smith's *Flaming Creatures*, a gay transvestite film already the victim of numerous bannings and obscenity charges. The Toronto morality squad (which had charged gallery owner Dorothy Cameron for her art exhibit Eros '65) turned up with the press but were foiled when the film failed to arrive from New York on time. In the United States, filmmakers were well served by the New York-based Film-Makers' Cooperative (established in 1962), which not only distributed every film submitted to it but also issued manifestos against censorship and commercial and other interferences with creativity.

Although experimental filmmaking developed later in Canada than in the United States, by 1964 it had evolved to such an extent that the Isaacs Art Gallery in Toronto could present several programs of Canadian experimental films in February and November. The Bohemian Embassy began experimental film screenings in 1965. By the following year, screenings of underground films from both the United States and Canada were an entrenched part of the alternative cultural scene in Toronto.

Whether Cronenberg was aware of these early stirrings of film activity in Toronto is unclear. Certainly he could not have seen the screenings of American underground films at the Bohemian Embassy in the fall of 1965. By then he was following in the path of other disillusioned university students: dropping out. Although he had been awarded the Gertrude Lawler Scholarship after finishing first in his class at University College, he was still drawn to the idea of being a novelist and convinced that academic studies could not teach him how to write. Perhaps inspired by his mentor, William Burroughs (who believed that travel was a stimulus to artistic creativity and change), he decided that he needed to see something of real life beyond his parochial Toronto background and left to live in Europe for a year.

Cronenberg based himself mainly in Copenhagen but also spent time in London during the heyday of the Beatles, the Rolling Stones, and the *outré* fashions of Carnaby Street. He told Bruce Martin in 1969 that he bought an old Volkswagen with no reverse gear and visited East Berlin, Yugoslavia, Istanbul, and Paris. In March he went to Hydra, but "It was freezing and Leonard Cohen was very sensibly in Montreal." He grew shoulder-length hair, adopted the new fashions, and enjoyed himself immensely. He met many other wanderers on personal odysseys of discovery, bound together by an emerging subculture of rock, pot, hatred of the United States, and, of course, hair. He found that life and opinions were much freer in Europe than in staid Toronto. However, he does not seem to have progressed much with his writing, being trapped still by the voices of Nabokov and Burroughs.

If he returned to Toronto not a little changed, so too was the Toronto to which he returned. The cultural scene was developing a vigorous life, shedding the elusive individuality that Rupert Brooke had described, its "subtly normal and obvious personality." Not the least of these changes was in the film scene. A cinematic culture was emerging in Toronto and elsewhere in Canada, led by young filmmakers undaunted by the apparent difficulties of making films. Many of these were in university milieus. After his return, Cronenberg was quickly attracted to the nascent film scene. Film would liberate him from his literary possession by Nabokov and Burroughs. He could find his own voice.

Watching David Cronenberg's first two short films today is to see barely a sketch of the themes and styles of his later films. Both *Transfer* and *From the Drain* are one-note films for two performers, somewhat surrealist in tone but technically awkward. Both have the off-centre humour that we associate with Cronenberg. Both touch on issues of science: *Transfer* is a dialogue between a psychiatrist and an obsessive former patient; *From the Drain* is a dialogue set in the future between two fully clothed men in a bathtub discussing biological mutations when a plant emerges from the drain and kills one of them. This latter film contains elements of Emergent Evolutionism and hints at a similar use of bathtub drains in *Shivers*. In *Transfer* there is perhaps a trace of comparable obsessive relationships that occur in later films such as *The Brood*.

If neither of these films is little more than a sketch for Cronenberg's later work, they do reflect their time and are similar to other student-made films. The sixties witnessed a boom in underground films, and, in Canada, many of them were made by university students. Fuelled by a contemporary passion for film, and in the (perhaps felicitous) absence of university film courses, students set about making their own independent films. These ranged in approach from straight narrative to experimental works inspired by the New York underground. Many of them focused on the lives and loves of young people. Others emphasized experimental imagery. Many broke sexual taboos and ran afoul of provincial censor boards. Some of the filmmakers involved went on to careers in film, and a few are now well-known names.

The first such student film was made in 1962 at L'Université de Montréal. The feature-length *Seul ou avec d'autres* was directed by Denys Arcand and Denis Héroux and involved many who, like the directors, were to play leading roles in the developing Quebec cinema. At the University of British Columbia in 1963,

Larry Kent, a fourth-year student, made the feature *The Bitter Ash* for $5,000 and launched the film on campus screenings across the country. Although screenings at UBC and McGill University were sold out, the film thereafter ran into censorship difficulties because of a seminude sex scene. Screenings at McMaster and Carleton Universities were halted by university officials, and the print was later seized by the Ontario Censor Board. However, the receipts from the screenings enabled Kent to finance a second feature, *Sweet Substitute*, in 1964. This film won critical praise, was shown at several festivals, and had a theatrical release. Kent went on to make several more stylized, expressionistic features.

In Ontario, student film activity was centred at the University of Toronto and McMaster University (though artists in London, including Jack Chambers and Greg Curnoe, also began making films in the midsixties). First was David Secter, a fourth-year English student at the University of Toronto, who began filming a feature, *Winter Kept Us Warm*, late in 1964. Secter had written a scathing review of *The Bitter Ash* for the *Toronto Daily Star* but was undoubtedly inspired by Kent's example to make a narrative feature film on a low budget. Initial financing was provided by the student council, and the cast and crew were all students. Although shooting was completed by the summer of 1965, editing was delayed because of lack of funds, and the film was only completed late in 1965 after it was invited to the Commonwealth Film Festival. It was subsequently selected for several other festivals and received a warm critical reception. Its story about a short but intense friendship between two male students was given added bite by implying a homosexual attraction between the two. In retrospect, its appeal lies as much in its honest, unpretentious approach as in its authentic sense of campus life in the midsixties. Secter made one more (unsuccessful) feature the following year before dropping out of filmmaking.

By late 1966, film activity in Toronto and Hamilton was reaching unprecedented levels. At McMaster University, regular screenings of underground films began in 1965, and the McMaster Film Board was created. Those involved included Peter Rowe,

Ivan Reitman, and founder John Hofsess, a "drop-in" nonstudent. Others involved included future comedian, Eugene Levy, and Dan Goldberg, who would be sound supervisor for *Shivers* and later a Hollywood screenwriter. Hofsess, somewhat older than the others, was undoubtedly the inspirational voice. He also wrote a five-part series of articles, "Revolution in Canadian Film," for the University of Toronto student newspaper that undoubtedly influenced developments there. Hofsess directed *Redpath 25* in 1966, a true underground film with psychedelic, sensuous images, split screen, and a sexual theme. He followed it a year later with a sequel, *Black Zero*, in which Cronenberg appears briefly in a nude scene. The two films comprised *Palace of Pleasure*, in which two images were simultaneously projected on a single screen. Peter Rowe began an active film and theatre career with a 1967 underground film, *Buffalo Airport Visions*, and continued with a feature film in 1970, *The Neon Palace*, a nostalgic tribute to the popular culture of the fifties and sixties. Ivan Reitman, now a well-established Hollywood producer and director of films such as *Ghostbusters*, *Legal Eagles*, and *Twins*, also began his career in 1967 with the McMaster Film Board by directing short films. He later produced and directed several low-budget features in Canada and was Cronenberg's producer for *Shivers*.

Hofsess also turned to feature filmmaking in 1969 when he wrote and directed the ambitious *The Columbus of Sex*, based on *My Secret Life*, a novel (or sexual memoir?) written by an anonymous Victorian author. The producers were Reitman and Goldberg. Hofsess's aim was to make a liberating film about sexuality in a visual, sensuous style. At its first screening (a private one at McMaster), the film was seized by police, and Hofsess, Reitman, and Goldberg were charged with making and exhibiting an obscene film. At their trial, Hofsess was acquitted on a technicality; Reitman and Goldberg were found guilty but fined only a token amount and placed on probation. However, by then Reitman had sold the rights to a United States distributor who added new footage and reedited it for release as *My Secret Life*. The original film (which, like *Palace of Pleasure*, was dual projection) has never been shown in public. But as one of those who saw it at a private screening, I can testify that it was a lusciously beautiful, sophisticated, almost meditative work. Although replete with erotic imagery, it was totally unexploitative. Had it been released, it would have been one of the highlights of the period of underground filmmaking.

Film activity at the University of Toronto in the midsixties was no less prolific, even though fewer career filmmakers emerged from the liveliness. Screenings of underground films began in 1965, and a film production club was set up. In the summer of 1966, Bob Fothergill, Sam Gupta, and Glenn McCauley made their first short films.

It was to this atmosphere of cinematic ferment that Cronenberg returned from Europe. He recalls that it was Secter's feature, *Winter Kept Us Warm*, that most impressed him, but it is impossible that he was unaware of the swirl of film activity in the region that was about to peak when he returned. What struck him about Secter's film was not that he knew the director (he didn't) but that it featured actors who were his friends. (They included Janet Amos, Iain Ewing, Joy Teperman, Henry Tarvainen, and Jack Messinger, all of whom went on to various careers in the arts and two of whom appeared in Cronenberg's films.) It also featured scenes and places that he recognized. Until then, he had thought of film as something inaccessible, coming from elsewhere. Suddenly, filmmaking seemed a real possibility. As he told Beard and Handling, "And it takes someone your own age or someone close to you to suddenly say, 'My God, I can do this — it's exciting.' And that's exactly what happened." The underground cinema offered him a way to bypass the Hollywood system and even to ignore the absence of any equivalent in Canada. It was unprecedented and liberating. It suggested, as he said to Rodley, that "you didn't have to carry someone else's [film] cans around for twenty years" before making your own film. "That was the beginning of my awareness of film as something that I could do, something that I had access to."

FIGURE 6

The filmmaker-aesthete shoots Stereo *in 1968.*

When he discovered film, David Cronenberg felt liberated from the literary influences that had stultified his novel-writing ambitions. He became aware, he told Rodley, that "There was something about the medium of film that just fitted my temperament like a glove." Characteristically, given his well-established preoccupation with figuring out how things work, he began with the technical aspects of filmmaking. He felt that writing a script would be the easy part. So he began reading encyclopaedias and *American Cinematographer* magazine in order to understand the workings of cameras, lenses, sound recording, and the editing process. He also began hanging around the Canadian Motion Picture Equipment Company, a camera-rental service. There he learned from professional cinematographers and, not least, from Janet Good, the company's feisty head. She was not only Cronenberg's first supporter but also a friend to many young filmmakers, allowing them to defer equipment-rental payments, sometimes even forgoing them entirely.

Cronenberg wrote a script for two performers and, in January 1966, set about filming *Transfer*. He did his own 16mm colour cinematography and editing; two friends played the roles of psychiatrist and patient while others (including Margaret Hindson, his future wife) handled the sound recording. In the manner of numerous underground films, it was a surrealist-influenced tale. In it a patient obsessed by his psychiatrist pursues him everywhere because he feels that the relationship is the only significant one he has had. Much of the film shows the two characters eating at a table in the middle of a snowy field with no explanation offered as to why they are there. Again in the manner of other underground films, it avoids straight narrative and plays with visual dislocations. Seen today, it is no more than what it was: a first attempt. Hindsight, however, might also point to the quirky psychological humour and to the anticipation of other obsessive relationships that occur in Cronenberg's later films.

On 4 November 1966, Glenn McCauley organized a screening of student underground films at the University of Toronto, bringing together films from McMaster and York Universities as well as the University of Toronto. Following that screening, at which many of the filmmakers met for the first time, Cronenberg and several other filmmakers decided to create the Film-Makers Co-operative of Canada (later renamed, and still active as, the Canadian Filmmakers Distribution Centre) modelled on the Film-Makers' Co-operative in New York. Its first directors were Bob Fothergill and Iain Ewing, another student filmmaker who had worked with David Secter and made the first of many independent films in 1967. The new film cooperative, however, did not become the primary centre of film activity but evolved mainly into a nonprofit distribution outlet. Instead, it was a commercial distribution company, Film Canada, and its associated theatre, Cinecity, that became the focal points for underground cinema.

Film Canada had been founded by Willem Poolman, a flamboyant, gay, Dutch-born entrepreneur and former lawyer with a passionate interest in non-Hollywood films. It specialized in distributing art films from Europe, Quebec, and English Canada as well as underground films from the United States. After meeting with John Hofsess of the McMaster Film Board, Poolman became a dedicated supporter of the burgeoning local underground scene. He helped to finance numerous independent films as well as the rental of space for the new film cooperative. More significantly, he provided the focal point for most of the independent filmmaking in the region.

Although Film Canada had the distribution rights to many nonmainstream films, there were few theatres in which to show them because of the control by the Odeon and Famous Players theatre chains. Poolman leased a former post-office building at the corner of Yonge and Charles Streets and converted it into Cinecity, a well-equipped film theatre that included facilities for independent filmmakers. During its five-year life, it became the Mecca for the Toronto film community. Regular presentations of commercial art films were interspersed with screenings of underground films. Cronenberg recalls that Poolman and Cinecity "had a very long and profound influence on all of us." Cronenberg was a familiar member of the audience, and he was one of those invited to private screenings of films that Poolman was previewing in order to decide whether to buy them. As he told William Beard and Piers Handling, "It . . . made us all feel like insiders as opposed to outsiders. And when you start to feel that you are an insider it helps with your sense of power. You feel you can actually do something rather than be just a spectator."

By far the most exciting event at Cinecity was Cinethon, a marathon festival of underground films programmed by Fothergill. Underground films were screened nonstop from the evening of Thursday 15 June until midnight Saturday 17 June 1967. Many of the leading lights of American underground cinema were present to introduce their films, and virtually every available local film was screened. Cronenberg recalls it as "a great event" in his life. He told Beard and Handling:

> I remember emerging to have croissants and coffee in the morning and saying, "This is art!" At about five in the morning the sun was just coming up, and we came out for a break and went back into the theatre for another four hours of films. My film was shown amongst all the others.

Although, he also recalled, without getting a particularly good response.

Cinecity continued regular film screenings until 1971, when Poolman's company ran into financial difficulties. It was taken over by Budge Crawley (of Crawley Films), who discarded all the underground films. The demise of Cinecity marked the end of a brief but exciting period in Toronto filmmaking. Its former home now houses a Wendy's franchise outlet.

Meanwhile, Cronenberg had made another short film. Shot in the summer of 1966, with Cronenberg again handling the 16mm camera and editing, *From the Drain*, like its predecessor, has two

41

characters and a restricted setting: in this case, a bathtub. Two fully clothed men sit in the dry tub discussing what seems to be a bizarre, futuristic war involving biological and chemical weapons that caused mutations. A plant comes out of the drain and strangles one of the men. The other takes the man's shoes and throws them in a closet already full of shoes. As Cronenberg described it to Beard and Handling, "So it's obvious that somewhere along the line there is a plot to get rid of all the veterans of that particular war so they won't talk about what they know." That conclusion is more evident in the telling than in the seeing, but as a film it was more technically adept than *Transfer*, marked by zany, black humour — and, of course, a sense of Emergent Evolutionism in its plant mutations. Sometimes it seems that there are more ideas in the film than can be comfortably contained in its fourteen-minute length. Cronenberg thinks of it as having been influenced by Samuel Beckett. However, it seems more comparable to the kind of sketch soon to be associated with *Monty Python's Flying Circus*.

Cronenberg remarked to Rodley that he found making these two short films "tremendously exciting" as well as "tremendously frustrating, because you're not able to get what you want." He had worked on them as essentially personal projects and was to continue this approach with his next two films. Because the underground cinema emphasized the personal approach, he never felt isolated. In fact, he felt very much a part of the emerging film community. "I remember summer nights," he told Rodley,

you'd stroll through various sections of town that were hippiefied and you'd find people screening films on sheets strung up on store fronts, and people sitting on the sidewalk watching. It was very exciting. Your film could be one of those, and you were part of it.

Cronenberg had also increasingly lost interest in academic studies, as had others in his milieu. He dropped out of honours

English and graduated in 1967 with a general BA. He was to spend the following months determining his next step.

Undoubtedly David Cronenberg was enjoying his life in 1967. He was part of a youthful film group that was creating an alternative to the establishment. He was an "insider" in a group that defined itself as an "outsider" in relation to that establishment. Although his two films had attracted little attention, he had the satisfaction of having proved to himself that he could handle filmmaking, that he had quickly acquired the necessary technical skills. He was, though, faced with the decision of what to do next. While it is impossible to know his thought processes at the time, it is not difficult to surmise. If his artistic ambitions were to be fulfilled, then he had to differentiate himself from his peers. He could hardly continue making small films like his first two. Even in the underground cinema, the films that stood out were the most audacious: in the boldness of their content (such as Kenneth Anger's films), or their visual richness (such as Stan Brakhage's films), or their formal experimentation (as in Andy Warhol's two-screen *Chelsea Girls* or in John Hofsess's two-screen *Palace of Pleasure*). Cronenberg, however, did not wish to copy these approaches, quite apart from the fact that none of them reflected his own sensibility.

At what point Cronenberg decided to make a feature-length film on the professional 35mm gauge is unclear. Certainly thoughts such as those above must have passed through his mind. His decision to use 35mm itself suggests this. Underground filmmakers used 16mm and Super 8mm films because they were accessible and relatively cheap. However, using them also limited audiences to venues such as art galleries and libraries. Using 35mm at least offered the potential for screenings in commercial movie theatres. It also automatically moved

43

Cronenberg into a different league than other underground filmmakers. It gave him a mark of distinction from his peers. Although the decision to make *Stereo* in 35mm may seem less remarkable in retrospect, it was a bold move for a twenty-five-year-old filmmaker with only two, largely ignored, short films to his credit. He himself said simply to Bruce Martin after the film's release: "The desire to make a film I could accept myself as a real film was compulsive."

Cronenberg's decision to use 35mm also imposed on him certain technical limitations. The 35mm Arriflex camera (which kind-hearted Janet Good was prepared to make available to him on a deferred rental basis) was noisy. This problem precluded shooting synchronous sound and dialogue. Cronenberg does not now recall whether the content of the film or the technical decision came first. However, it seems most likely that he opted for 35mm and wrote-off synchronous sound, deciding to develop a script that could be shot with voice-over narration added later.

He submitted a script proposal to the Canada Council only to discover that there was no category for film projects in 1967. (One was added the following year.) So he resubmitted his proposal as a literary one, requesting funding to write a Nabokov-style novel. He received $3,500, which he used to establish a film-processing credit at a Toronto laboratory. He called his production unit Emergent Films, with the thought that his films would, he told Rodley, be "these emergent creatures that would be unprecedented and not able to have been predicted." As with his short films, he was a one-person crew and later edited the film himself. He thought of himself as an isolationist. He told Beard and Handling:

But I felt very private about the work I was doing, and the projects I was thinking of were just not communicable to anyone else. It never occurred to me to get help other than from a few friends, and the actors were also friends and acquaintances.

FIGURE 7

Filming Ron Mlodzik for Stereo.

Stereo was shot in black and white in the late summer of 1968 at the Scarborough College campus of the University of Toronto. The college's sterile, alienating architecture (unfortunately common in many institutional buildings of the sixties and aptly described as "Brutalist") became an expressive backdrop for the theme. The story is set in some unidentified future. A group of young adults has volunteered for an experiment in artificially induced telepathy organized by the Canadian Academy for Erotic Enquiry. The aim is to test the ESP and sexuality assumptions proposed by "aphrodisiast and theorist" Luther Stringfellow. One of his ideas suggests that telepathists will be the prototype of "three-dimensional man." The participants are isolated in a stark, modern building while unseen researchers observe their behaviour on television monitors. Using this basic story premise and an outline of the seven characters involved, Cronenberg allowed the film to evolve during shooting. The voice-over narration (supposedly research reports of the experiment) was written afterward. The final cost was about $8,500, most of which was in deferred payments for equipment and processing.

The film was completed in early 1969, and Cronenberg prepared to launch it (through Poolman's Film Canada) in a major way. He did not intend to allow this film to vanish into the underground as his short films had. He began showing it to critics and prepared to enter it in film festivals. It garnered several positive advance reports and reviews from Toronto and Montreal critics. Not the least of its admirers (ironically, in view of later events) was Robert Fulford, who described it in *Saturday Night* as "an exceptionally elegant dream." It had its official première at the National Arts Centre in Ottawa on 23 June 1969, and it was later presented at the Edinburgh and Adelaide festivals. World distribution rights were bought by New York-based International Film Archives in August for $10,000, and the company also took a $5,000 option on Cronenberg's next film. In September, it was the only Canadian film included in the science-fiction series held at New York's Museum of Modern Art. Cronenberg could hardly have hoped for such an immediate and encouraging reception. His audacity had paid off. As British critic Tony Rayns wrote, *Stereo* was "a true 'original,' defying categorisation." *Stereo* has a "subtitle," "TILE 3b of a CAEE EDUCATIONAL MOSAIC," followed by:

WARNING
All CAEE Educational Audiovisual Tiles designate
SAVC FIELD: OT are exposure restricted in
accordance with the provisions of the
CANADIAN PLASTIC FORMS ACT

The sham serious tone here anticipates the film's simulated documentary style. It also sets the tone for its mocking of the supposed objectivity of the documentary style (and, not least, Canada's hallowed contributions to it). The narrators' unfeeling voices often describe events at odds with what we see in the images. The unemotional, disconnected narration (with its absurd mixture of real and invented scientific jargon) contrasts with the sensuous plasticity of the imagery, the dreamlike action, and Cronenberg's formalized use of space within the frame. The film also clearly anticipates the thematic concerns of his later work, not least those of dehumanized sexuality and the rupture of the mind-body link. Many of the ideas about telepathy recur in *Scanners*; the notion of "omnisexuality," in which psychic and social inhibitions are eliminated by a new sexuality, is central to *Shivers*. *Stereo* also includes the requisite underground-film sex scenes and, what critic Joe Medjuck called, "a lovely group grope in which . . . the participants actually look as though they're having fun."

More to the point, perhaps, *Stereo* is Cronenberg's first attempt to explore some of the ideas of William Burroughs. The induced telepathy is analogous to Burroughs's drug-induced psychic autonomy: both are supposed to give new insights into mind and reality and to help the ego break free of social conditioning. As with Burroughs, the researchers in *Stereo* reveal to us that artificially induced mental freedom produces new physical and social bondages and a reinforcement of the separation of mind and body. The experiments at the academy recall those that Burroughs describes, in a section of *The Job*, in an academy that is "all glass and steel shining in the cold northern sunlight." And the narrators' nonjudgemental point of view is reminiscent of Burroughs's approach in *Junkie*.

The parallels with Burroughs are too close to be accidental. Yet the film is not all comparable to Burroughs's writings. (We might except some of the phrasing in the narration; phrases such as Burroughs's "oceanic organismal subconscious body thinking" have their parallels in the film.) While some aspects of the Burroughsian universe are in *Stereo*, its style and structure are very much Cronenberg's own. The only filmic influence that we might locate is the work of French director Alain Resnais, particularly in the precise stagings and use of space in films such as *Last Year at Marienbad*. But even that seems more an indirect than a direct influence.

Stereo was the film that established Cronenberg's career. In the fall of 1969, soon after the film's release, he described himself to Kaspars Dzeguze as having reached "mystical being," the point at which he was accepted into the world of film. "Suddenly, you exist — you can go to people involved in film and approach them on equal terms." His name had been buried in *Stereo*'s end credits; for his new film, though, he felt confident enough to announce at its beginning: "A David Cronenberg Film."

CRIMES OF THE FUTURE

David Cronenberg had started work on his next film before the release of *Stereo*. He had planned to film it in black and white, but *Stereo*'s success meant that he could think more ambitiously and shoot it in colour. Funding for the film's $15,000 budget came from the International Film Archives and from the newly established Canadian Film Development Corporation. The CFDC was supposed to stimulate the development of the Canadian film industry, but there was disagreement about how best to achieve this. Should new directors be supported, or only commercially viable projects? The practical consequence of this policy debate was that the CFDC, for its first few years, supported both before adopting commercial viability as a principal element of its policy. As Cronenberg later remarked to Chris Rodley, ". . . I slipped in under the wire"; "[*Crimes of the Future*] was maybe the first and last experimental film they put money into." He had, however, not got funding by default. He had been active in promoting his work as what he termed, to Bruce Martin and others, "real feature films" that were eligible for funding.

The film's story is set in some unidentified future, a time of genetic mutations, in which millions of postpubescent females have died from Rouge's Malady. Events are again dominated by an "absent" theorist: in this case the mad dermatologist Antoine Rouge, discoverer of the malady. Rouge's ardent disciple, Adrian Tripod, describes his various encounters as he drifts uncomprehendingly from place to place and into increasingly absurd and anarchic situations. In contrast to the pseudodocumentary structure of *Stereo*, the new film was a well-structured quest narrative. In addition to the voice-over narration, Cronenberg added a second sound track composed of underwater sounds.

Cronenberg again handled cinematography and editing. The cast of friends and acquaintances was much larger. Back from the earlier film were Ron Mlodzik (as Adrian Tripod), filmmaker Iain Ewing, Jack Messinger, and Paul Mulholland. Also in the cast were filmmaker Don Owen, Willem Poolman from Film Canada, journalists Kaspars Dzeguze, Bruce Martin, and Brian Linehan, as well as friend Norman Snider, with whom Cronenberg would later travel to Hollywood and with whom he collaborated on *Dead Ringers*. Cronenberg thinks that both *Crimes of the Future* and *Stereo* were conditioned by the presence of Mlodzik, whom he described to Beard and Handling as "a very elegant gay scholar" with a "sort of medieval gay sensibility, which I like a lot. . . . . [H]ow directly that connects with my own sexuality or not, it certainly connects very directly with my aesthetic sense of his space and his presence in those films." There are other similarities between *Crimes of the Future* and *Stereo*: sexuality, genetic mutations, the mind-body link, and the use of abstract, formalized decor and Brutalist architecture. Both use black humour to great effect. They are almost wickedly inventive. They can be equally related to ideas of William Burroughs, not least in their use of pseudoscience and popularized science as mythology and metaphor. Cronenberg's diseases and "creative cancers" are as connected here to Burroughs's idea of cancer as virus in *Naked Lunch* as they are to his own later *Shivers* and *Rabid*. Although both films could properly be called science fiction, they owe virtually nothing to that film genre, reminding us more of literary influences: Burroughs, of course; Brecht in the "epic" quality of the drama and the use of alienation effects; Nabokov in the distancing of voice from image; even Jorge Luis Borges in the narration's allusiveness and dry wit.

In these films we are introduced to Cronenberg's liking for strange names for his characters and institutions. (Featured in *Crimes of the Future* are The Institute for Neo-Venereal Disease and the Oceanic Podiatry Group.) Equally prominent in both films is his play with real and fake scientific jargon. Cronenberg told David Chute in 1980 that he thinks of this play as "affectionate mimicry, rather than parody." Both traits continue in his later films: for example, Brian O'Blivion in *Videodrome* and The Somafree Institute of Psychoplasmics in *The Brood*. Cronenberg claims that, unlike Nabokov, he does not intend his names to be read as literary puns and that, however bizarre, he discovers them all in real life.

Both films also benefited from Cronenberg's cinematography, especially in terms of the remarkable use of colour in *Crimes of the Future*. They are far from the camerawork usually seen in underground films and revealed a born filmmaker. He later told John Colapinto: "Until I did them, I didn't know if I had an eye — a *feel* for composition and movement. It was a visceral thing.

I just *knew* when something was right or wrong, and I still do." Although he was not able to photograph his later films, he still retains this visual sensibility. "My eye for composition is very specific," he said in an interview with Paul Sammon. "This is no joke: I feel physically ill when I look through a lens and things aren't properly composed." In *Crimes of the Future* he made considerable use of unedited long takes, precisely designing the visual impact of each shot.

Some critics, Sammon for instance, who admire Cronenberg's later films have dismissed these first two as "arty, overly pretentious, and statically boring," interesting only in their anticipation of the thematic concerns of his "professional work." They are, however, more than mere apprenticeship films. They are perfect little works, complete in themselves, skilfully balancing modernist narrative influences and popular science fiction. Unlike many underground films of the time, they remain eminently watchable (if less immediately accessible than his commercial films).

Crimes of the Future was completed in February 1970. Surprisingly, given the positive reception of *Stereo*, it was largely ignored by Canadian critics. It was, though, well received in Europe, especially in London and Paris, where it garnered numerous ecstatic reviews. He later met one of the admiring French critics who told him, he related to Rodley, "I was convinced after you made those films that you would never make another."

Having completed the film, Cronenberg had no new project ready to pursue. He was now married to Margaret Hindson, whom he had met in university and with whom he had lived for some time. He was not sure that he wanted to continue filmmaking in the same noncommercial vein. He had applied for, and received, a Canada Council grant that freed him for a year from the pressures of an immediate project. Distance from Canada had once before allowed him to rethink his direction. It was to do so again. For the next year, Cronenberg lived in the south of France. When he returned to Canada, he had emerged completely from the underground. He was again an outsider.

"ETONNE-MOI!"

"Astonish me!" was the comment attributed to Russian impresario, Sergei Diaghilev, by Jean Cocteau, who had asked him how best to win his praise. If David Cronenberg had surprised the Canadian film community by his sudden emergence from the 16mm short-film ghetto, he was to astonish — and even shock — it with his next film. *Shivers* was to put him at the centre of controversy and even notoriety. This modestly budgeted horror film became the most commercially successful film in which the Canadian Film Development Corporation had invested. It also became the centre of a storm of controversy over the appropriateness of Canadian tax dollars being used to produce such a "tasteless" film. Cronenberg had certainly succeeded in drawing attention to his distinctiveness whether or not he had consciously set out to do so.

He was well aware in 1970–71 that his career was at a critical juncture. He wondered where underground cinema and his role in relation to it were going. Did he want to continue making films that gave him no real income, that were well received critically but seen by only a handful of people? Should he continue as the romantic, solitary artist in the manner of William Burroughs? Or should he define himself as a professional filmmaker and, inevitably, commit himself to working in the commercial film industry? Interestingly, while completing *Crimes of the Future*, he still preferred the solitary-artist role. In an article for *Film* magazine, he complained that the CFDC was "trying to institute Hollywood-type production" and that it was "taking the industry part of it to heart more than the film part."

Cronenberg lived for almost a year in Tourettes-sur-Loup, a small village in the south of France. Several factors were to play a role in his final decision. He again tried writing a novel, only to learn that it was no easier for him than it had been before. He destroyed the draft and has since confined his writing to film scripts. He was interested in sculpture and even tried his hand at

FIGURE 8

Eye to the camera, staging Shivers.

one that he called *Surgical Instrument for Operating on Mutants* — a curious anticipation of the instruments in *Dead Ringers*. Film, however, remained at the centre of his interests. He bought a 16mm camera and made three "fillers" for television: two- to three-minute impressionistic documentaries intended to fill what would otherwise be dead airtime. One was on Tourettes itself, the second on Montreal sculptor Jim Ritchie, who was then living in France, and the third was *Letter from Michelangelo*, with narration drawn from Michelangelo's writings. They were the first works for which Cronenberg was paid a commercial fee, a fact that no doubt influenced his evolving decision to work in mainstream film. They proved that he could actually earn money at his profession. When he returned to Canada the following year, he made six more television fillers.

Cronenberg was also aware that the era of underground cinema was coming to a close. The signs were plentiful. There was the 1970 obscenity trial of John Hofsess's *Columbus of Sex* and its reediting for commercial sale in the United States as a soft-core porno movie. Willem Poolman's Film Canada and Cinecity were floundering and were sold in 1971. Most of Cronenberg's underground filmmaking friends had abandoned independent production. Some dropped out of film entirely; others joined the CBC. The few independent features that were made (including Iain Ewing's *Kill* and Peter Rowe's *Neon Palace*) attracted only modest critical attention and virtually no commercial receipts. Cronenberg recalled the period to Chris Rodley:

We were now in a sort of half-life, the afterglow of the 1960s. Charles Manson and Woodstock had happened. Bobby Kennedy had been shot. It was another era. . . . I knew that despite the fact I now had a family to support, I didn't want to do any of that other stuff.

His visit to the film festival at Cannes in 1971 was decisive. Initially he was appalled by the commercial hucksterism and self-indulgent displays of wealth, and he fled back to Tourettes after only half a day. There he realized that if he wanted to be a professional, ". . . I'm going to have to come to terms with the Cannes film festival. . . . I forced myself to go back there." He discovered that, when one approached the festival with a sense of humour, it could actually be enjoyable. The CFDC let him sleep on a couch in their offices at the Ritz Carlton Hotel. "The two visits to Cannes were entirely different," he further told Beard and Handling. "Even though the festival was the same, I was very different. And I realized that, yes, I was willing to do what was necessary to make commercial movies."

It was a crucial decision, and its implications were clear to Cronenberg. He realized that it meant the end of filmmaking as a personal act of creation with total control over script, cinematography, and editing. He recalled his feelings at the time to Beard and Handling:

I thought in terms of making a movie instead of a film. I would have a crew that was paid for by a producer who was in it because he felt the film would make money and who had plans to distribute it. . . . I would no longer be able to make it totally in private without any consideration whether they liked what I was doing or not.

He must also have been aware that the decision to move into the mainstream would be another break in the chain that had bound him to William Burroughs.

At the same time, Cronenberg's wife Margaret was moving in something of an opposite direction. Soon after their daughter Cassandra was born in 1972, Margaret began exploring various religious beliefs. "Like a lot of people in that era, she went on an inner search," friend Norman Snider told John Colapinto in 1986. "It led her to every organization around. David is a rationalist. He lives a fairly private, isolated life, and she was trying to find some sense of community among these various cults that he had no time for at all." A breakup seemed inevitable, and, within a few years after their return from France, they were to separate and eventually divorce.

Cronenberg had already lined up a commercial project when he returned to Toronto in late spring 1971. Norman Snider had written a short drama for television. Set in the near future following a civil war, *Secret Weapons* is the story of a drug-company monopoly that tries to force a former researcher to reveal the results of his experiments with aggression stimulants. The theme and ideas are so close to those in Cronenberg's earlier work that it seems likely the two friends jointly developed at least the story outline. The CBC commissioned Cronenberg's company, Emergent Films, to produce the film for Program X, a series designed to include unusual or controversial subject matter as well as to encourage new writing and directing talent. Cronenberg both directed and photographed the twenty-seven-minute film, which was broadcast on CBC Television in June 1972. Among the cast were old friends Ron Mlodzik and Bruce Martin, as well as Norman Snider; there was even a role for Michael Spencer, executive director of the CFDC and an admirer of Cronenberg's work since *Stereo*. Although a short television drama was hardly the commercial mainstream, Cronenberg had proved that he could work to a budget, fulfil a contract, and meet commercial constraints. The CBC later hired him to direct more television dramas.

Cronenberg was also pursuing his goal with the same tenacious sense of purpose and limitless self-confidence that he had brought to his first 35mm features. He started writing a feature film script as well as showing his work to commercial producers. He had no intention of sitting around, waiting to be offered work.

It was not an easy time to enter the Canadian film industry. Cronenberg was aware that other filmmakers (such as Sidney Furie and Norman Jewison) had felt it necessary to leave the country to have a career. He did not share that feeling but, as he told Rodley, not "out of a fierce sense of nationalism. I just thought that I should be able to make films in Canada." In the sixties many feature films had been made as personal projects of their directors. By the early seventies, the CFDC was having an impact on the film industry and the kinds of projects being made, but the cadre of commercial producers essential to a film industry was only slowly emerging. Most Canadian features had difficulty getting screenings in theatres controlled by the Famous Players and Odeon chains. There were fierce debates over the best means of breaking this deadlock. More daunting for Cronenberg, perhaps, was that influential Canadian critics preferred to admire films in the realist mode, considering them "characteristically Canadian." (There were other films being made, but critics tended to ignore them.) For Cronenberg, who thought of his films as "cinema of the imagination," this must have been a disturbing tendency. Yet, interestingly, it also reinforced his "outsider" status.

In his travels around production companies, Cronenberg encountered Cinépix, a Montreal distribution and production company founded by André Link, a francophone European Jew, and John Dunning, whom Cronenberg described to Rodley as "totally WASP." They had established themselves as a major force in Quebec's commercial film industry with the 1969 release of *Valérie*, a soft-core porno film that managed to combine sexual frankness, sentimentality, and Catholic morality. It cost only $99,000 to produce, grossed over $1.5 million, and spawned numerous imitators in Quebec — and a genre that became known as "maple-syrup porno." Cinépix was also one of the few companies in Canada with any continuity of production, and Cronenberg decided that he liked their sensibility. Critics and other serious filmmakers might have considered their films beneath contempt, "But," Cronenberg later told Rodley, "for me these were real movies, no question about it. These were movies that started to do stuff that I wouldn't mind doing, though maybe not in the same way." He approached Cinépix to audition for a new maple-syrup porno film (*Loving and Laughing*) that they were planning. He showed his films to John Dunning with some trepidation and was relieved to discover that the "very gentle and sweet and very encouraging" Dunning actually liked them. He shot a screen test for the film, bringing with him Iain Ewing to audition for the male lead role. (The underground network of mutual support was still active.) It was the first time that Cronenberg had been in a film studio. He recalls shooting a scene between a couple on a garden swing by setting the camera at a bizarre, low angle. Neither he nor Ewing was hired. However, a contact had been made, and it was to Cinépix that Cronenberg returned with his first commercial feature script.

Cronenberg has often been asked in interviews whether he consciously decided to write a script in the horror genre. He has always denied it. His denial is credible, given that *Shivers* owes little to generic models (other than the comparable attempt to affect an audience) and that it reflects the images of Burroughs more than those of the traditional horror film.

The script that Cronenberg began writing after his return from France was originally called "Satyr's Tongue" and then "Orgy of the Blood Parasites." He later felt that the latter title was too reminiscent of fifties Hollywood horror films and renamed it *The Parasite Murders*, the title under which it was first released. As he was writing, his father was dying. "It started as colitis," Cronenberg told Colapinto in 1986, "and became a very bizarre inability of the body to process calcium. His bones started to become brittle. He would turn over in bed and break ribs." His father's condition did not mean that the script was in any way autobiographical. It simply made Cronenberg "aware of my own mortality in an incredibly acute and emotional and close-to-home way. To have someone you love and respect and are close to die — slowly — is a horrible thing." He also witnessed the disintegration of the warm and close family relationships in which he had grown up. He recalled this situation for Katherine Govier in 1979: "He resented my mother because he was dying and she wasn't, and she resented having to take care of him. I remember him saying to me that he didn't see why he should have to die and I should live. His body was sick; he said he wanted to have my body." When his father died in 1973, Cronenberg was devastated and literally felt haunted by his spirit. He was later to say that all horror springs from the Latin phrase *Timor mortis conturbat mea*: "The fear of death disturbs me." This script was only the first of many that would explore coming to terms with death — and its mirror image, the meaning of life.

The script was also influenced by William Burroughs, especially *Naked Lunch*. Cronenberg felt driven, he admitted to Colapinto, by the Burroughsian aesthetic "to show the unshowable, to speak the unspeakable." The central image of the parasites ("bugs" as they were called during shooting) started with a dream in which a *thing* emerged from a man's mouth as he was lying in bed with his wife. There is such a scene in the film. (Cronenberg has told slightly different versions of this dream, including one to Stephen Chesley in which the thing crawled out of his own mouth. We might wonder whether this "dream" was not simply astute promotion.) Cronenberg later said to Paul Sammon that "It satisfied me enormously to invent a new creature. . . . The bugs came out of my childhood fascination with the microscopic, with insects and so on." The image of the bugs was later cloned for *Alien*. There is also an extreme concern with bodily functions from vomiting to bleeding. Parasites emerge from bathtub drains (shades of *From the Drain*) and slither between the legs of a woman, or pop out of people's mouths, or burst through a man's stomach. It was extreme and horrific imagery, like nothing ever seen on the screen. Cronenberg later told Sammon that it was part of "the old, you know, 'astonish me' gambit. We're talking about grossness, but that's the same thing. . . . Anyway, I think an artist is supposed to be extreme."

The script recounts the story of the inhabitants of an upscale apartment complex who find themselves being taken over by personality-altering parasites that make them sexually aggressive and violent. The strange disease passing from resident to resident puzzles the head of the building's medical clinic until he connects it with the suicide/murder of medical researcher Emil Hobbes and his mistress. Believing that humans had lost touch with their physical natures, Hobbes had implanted in his mistress a parasite that was a combination of aphrodisiac and venereal disease; finding it uncontrollable, he has killed his mistress and

59

then himself. The parasites quickly possess all the residents and then seem about to spread beyond the apartment building.

Cronenberg told Rodley that "It was a natural thing for me to write, and wasn't the slightest bit calculated. It fitted right in with the kind of writing I'd been doing my whole life, but it was a horror film." In thinking of it as a film, he was also certain, he told Beard and Handling, that the parasites could not be depicted "off-camera because nobody would know what was going on. . . . I was creating things that there was no way of suggesting because it was not common currency of the imagination. It had to be shown or else not done."

Cronenberg submitted the script to several producers, but only John Dunning at Cinépix liked it. It combined a horror theme with the sex staple they had successfully exploited; and, not least, it could be made on a low budget. For Cinépix it offered the potential of breaking into world markets, especially that of the United States. Dunning and André Link took the script to the CFDC where it was immediately rejected. Rumour, probably unfounded, hinted that the CFDC had invented an on-the-spot "policy" decision not to fund any horror films, even though it had already invested in several films that included sex and violence. CFDC executive director Michael Spencer later claimed to journalist Robert Martin that the CFDC "didn't exactly reject it. We said the script needed changes." In any case, Cronenberg's "breakthrough" project had floundered. He had lined up no other work. The two years that it took for the CFDC to change its mind were to become the most frustrating ones of his life.

"YOU HAVE TO BE PREPARED TO ENDURE"
— Cronenberg on William Burroughs

In fact, the period following Cronenberg's return from France was a lean and hungry one by anyone's measure. Apart from the one CBC directing job and a few television fillers, he did not work in his profession. He says now that he cannot remember how he and Margaret survived — though he did work for a time as a clerk at Sam the Record Man. Their marriage, however, was already crumbling. It disintegrated totally when Margaret later left him for Stephen Zeifman, one of Cronenberg's high-school friends and an actor in *Crimes of the Future*. Cronenberg seems to have borne him no ill will; he moved in with, and eventually married, Stephen's sister Carolyn. However, the later battle with Margaret over custody of their daughter Cassandra was to form the motivation for the script of *The Brood*.

In 1973, Cinépix brought in Ivan Reitman to help with Cronenberg's feature-film project. Reitman, a former underground filmmaker from the McMaster Film Board, had made a name for himself as producer of low-budget films such as *Cannibal Girls* and *Foxy Lady* and of Broadway shows such as Doug Henning's *The Magic Show*. Although the project remained stalled, Reitman was eventually to prove an ideal and supportive producer for Cronenberg's first commercial venture.

By early 1974, Cronenberg was desperate. He decided to tout for work, or at least support, in Hollywood. Because Roger Corman, the legendary producer and director of numerous low-budget cult films, had reacted warmly to his script, Corman became the ostensible reason for the trip. Norman Snider, a friend since university and sometime collaborator who was also struggling to establish himself as a writer, agreed to go with Cronenberg. Snider later wrote a playful account of their trip for *Saturday Night* magazine in which he describes them as *"The Bobbsey Twins Visit L.A."* They never met Corman, but Snider amusingly describes several close encounters. They did meet many Canadians who were not encouraging about cultural prospects in Canada. Among them was Lorne Michaels, former CBC producer and future producer of *Saturday Night Live*. Michaels told them: "We thought we were going to be the first generation that was going to be able to stay home . . . and *do* it. . . . But it didn't happen. You're going to have to come down here and so will your kids." Everything they heard and saw seemed to remind them of the old Canadian adage that "they'll reject you till you go somewhere else and make something happen. Then they won't be able to love you enough." Cronenberg himself joined in the litany of grievances, complaining of bureaucratic hassles at the CFDC and the absurd process of decision-making by committees. He was rebuked by Moses Znaimer, visiting Los Angeles from Toronto's CITY-TV. Znaimer told Cronenberg that the problem was not Canada; it was his trying to make feature films when everyone knew that they were a waste of time. Cronenberg, he continued, should become an accountant or a plumber because he had been unemployed for the better part of three years, and all for a possible ninety minutes on a screen somewhere. This depressing atmosphere culminated in Cronenberg's discovery that Cinépix had offered his script to a Hollywood director. He recalled the moment to Rodley: "I just went insane. Cinépix desperately wanted the script, but they didn't want me to direct, for obvious reasons. To come 3,000 miles to discover this betrayal! So I went back to Toronto really angry."

We might wonder whether that trip to Los Angeles did not reinforce Cronenberg's well-known insistence on working in Canada. Having been told that it was impossible, his stubborn self-confidence would urge him toward proving them wrong. Perhaps others could not make it, but *he* could. He would later remember Znaimer's remarks in Los Angeles when he created the character of Max Renn, the video-oriented, fictitious TV-station owner in *Videodrome*.

In any case, the fates were on Cronenberg's side, as they had been before in his career changes. When he returned to Toronto, there was a message saying that the CFDC had finally agreed to invest in the production of his script. Few people know what influenced the change of mind. Cronenberg speculated that it was CFDC executive director Michael Spencer himself. Spencer had liked Cronenberg's earlier work, saying to Robert Martin, "I think he's a good filmmaker. His previous work has shown that." Spencer likely concluded that *Shivers* would be a chance for Cronenberg to prove himself, one way or another. As Cronen-

FIGURE 9

Directing on the set of Shivers.

berg said simply to Rodley, the CFDC's decision marked "the beginning of my career as a movie-maker, and the end of my career as a film-maker."

MAKING *SHIVERS*

Production of *The Parasite Murders* was set to begin in Montreal in mid-August 1974. The budget was minuscule: approximately $180,000, of which $75,000 had been invested by the CFDC. Cronenberg has never forgotten his first professional production meeting. He "was stricken with the most profound melancholy," he told Chris Rodley. Although he didn't understand it at the time, "it was an incredible sense of loss: this was no longer mine. It was everybody's, a shared event. It was goodbye to a certain kind of filmmaking, where you do everything, if you can get a couple of friends to help."

Cronenberg had to bluff his way through that production meeting as well as the fifteen-day shoot. Several years later he recollected the experience to Paul Sammon:

> . . . I didn't know what an A.D. (assistant director) was, or what a production manager or gaffer did. . . . Everybody who worked on that film had made more movies than I had, and there I was writing and directing it. I was completely off balance all the way through the shoot in terms of working with professionals, in terms of not knowing what a sound mix or fx [effects] track was. . . .

Perhaps Cronenberg's most difficult adjustment was in terms of the cinematography, which he had always handled himself. He was horrified when he saw the first day's rushes. Nothing was on the screen as he had envisioned it. He told Stephen Chesley after the film was released: "For the first time in my life I said 'Gee maybe I can't do this.'" He had never felt like that before. Fortuitously, he saw the second and third days' rushes at the same time and realized that they were improving, day by day. His confidence returned as he learned to understand and manage the industrial filmmaking machine. Yet he continued to worry, as he noted to Sammon, whether he "had anything that would add up to a movie." Reitman was a major figure of support. Cronenberg said to Rodley that Reitman "was nothing but astonishing, and always knew what he wanted. I wavered at a certain point. He never did. He knew entertainment, commercial film-making." (Cronenberg later realized that Cinépix's adaptive response to his own inexperience was to surround him with more experienced people.)

The production was based in a high-rise apartment complex on Nuns' Island. The building is not as isolated as it appears in the film's opening sequence, a pseudo real-estate commercial extolling the virtues of "Starliner Towers." Photos of the island were retouched to replace the numerous other buildings with greenery. The plushly anonymous setting was an appropriate parallel to the similarly alienating environments that Cronenberg had used in the earlier films. He lived there during the production, as did many members of the crew, and told David Chute in 1980 that "it drove us *crazy*." He described Nuns' Island to Sammon as "very lifeless and soul[l]ess. It wasn't a community that grew in any organic way. Some company just imposed it, and people were supposed to move in." With his typical sense of humour, he told Chute that the film's characters had been *"liberated"* from their environment, "and to that extent I'm definitely on the side of the disease."

The only way the budget could cover Cronenberg's living in the complex was if his apartment doubled as a special-effects workroom. Also, because there was no money for sets, the production was dependent on the goodwill of people living in the complex. Signs were posted in the elevators asking people to loan their apartments — and there were several eager offers. With minimal adaptations, the donated apartments became the film's sets, except for a few of the more violent scenes, which were shot in vacant rooms.

FIGURE 10

On the set of Fast Company.

The cast was mainly Canadian, including Susan Petrie (a presence in numerous Canadian features of the time) and Ron Mlodzik in a supporting role. The two exceptions were Lynn Lowry, whom Cronenberg had seen in a George Romero horror film, and Barbara Steele, then famous as the "Queen of Italian horror films." Dealing with professional actors became another part of his "baptism of fire," not the least because the low budget meant that dialogue scenes had to be staged so that they were easy to shoot.

Cronenberg designed the image of the parasites, using a medical illustrator to give them an authentic appearance. Because there were no special-effects technicians in Canada, Joe Blasco was brought in from Hollywood. Although Cronenberg played little part in the choice of Blasco, he found him "totally ingenious and brilliant," capable of developing remarkable effects cheaply from easily available objects such as balloons and pieces of wire. "Joe was the master of fiddly, conceptual stuff," he told Rodley, "and he certainly knew his chemistry: you don't smear KY jelly on that foam because it will eat it away. . . . Conceptually he was wonderful too, and also very funny and intense."

With shooting completed by mid-September, the film moved into postproduction, and Cronenberg again learned hard lessons in terms of editing a commercial feature film. Because the emphasis had been on special effects and not on dialogue scenes, he found himself working with minimal footage and therefore limited choices in the editing room. When he saw the first rough cut, he was as depressed as he had been on the first day of shooting. "I had taken great care with continuity," he told Chesley,

> but I completely lost sight of the pace of the thing. Ivan wasn't involved in the first cut — he's very canny and knows when to be absent — and he's very good at insuring that a narrative line works. He saw what was wrong, and helped us edit. It's not every producer who can do that and not be a nuisance and be effective.

Release of the film was set for October 1975 in Montreal in both English and French versions. The English release title was *The Parasite Murders*, the French *Frissons* ("Shivers"); the greater commercial success of the French version then led to the title change of the English version. By the date of general release, Cinépix had sold the rights (mostly at the 1975 Cannes Film Festival) to so many countries that a full return on its production costs was guaranteed. It went on to gross some $5 million worldwide and won the Grand Prix at a Spanish festival of fantasy films. However, more was brewing for Cronenberg than simple congratulations on creating a commercial success.

"WHAT ARE WE GOING TO DO ABOUT CRONENBERG?"

In the summer of 1975, David Cronenberg arranged a private screening of *Shivers* for Robert Fulford, editor of *Saturday Night* magazine, who was also its film critic under the name of Marshall Delaney. Fulford had written an enthusiastic review of *Stereo*. Somewhat naïvely, Cronenberg assumed that Fulford would see the parallels between the two films. This was not to be. In his two-and-a-half page vitriolic review, highlighted on the cover, Fulford avoided, except implicitly, all mention of Cronenberg's earlier work. He did acknowledge "certain themes borrowed from avant-garde literature." But what had been a virtue in *Stereo* became in *Shivers* mere cynical exploitation designed to allow the director to retain "a certain self-respect." Fulford's review was headlined, "You Should Know How Bad This Film Is. After All, You Paid for It."

It was published in the September 1975 issue — prior to the film's release. It conditioned much of the film's critical reception in Canada, with most reviewers explicitly or implicitly addressing issues that Fulford raised about "excessively violent and perverted" films in general and the "impossible to convey" badness of *Shivers* in particular. Some, such as Jamie Portman, agreed with Fulford, arguing that, despite the box-office success, the film was "impossible to defend as art or even as a good film." Others wrote that though the film was gross, in bad taste, and horrible, it was supposed to be. It was "well made, imaginative trash," Dane Lanken wrote; it was "so funny-scary awful," picturing "all those dreams you wouldn't tell anybody . . . about," Natalie Edwards noted. For many reviewers, it seemed simply a question of whether one was for or against "bad taste." More temperate critics, such as Robert Martin, set it alongside other horror movies, arguing that "Shivers is a good horror film because it succeeds admirably in what it sets out to do, to revolt and disgust."

Had Fulford only written his opinion of the film, probably no one but the makers would have been agitated by his article. Cronenberg himself said to Chesley that he accepted Fulford's response but found it "too bad he couldn't have had that reaction and understood that it was a valid thing for a film to do." Fulford, however, used his distaste for the film to launch an attack on the policies of the CFDC. *Shivers*, he wrote, "is an atrocity, a disgrace to everyone connected with it — including the taxpayers. The question it raises is an old one now . . . : should we subsidize junk (or worse than junk) in order to create an 'industry' that will also, possibly, produce indigenous and valuable feature films?" He quoted extensively from Judy LaMarsh, the secretary of state responsible for the act that established the CFDC in 1967. He contrasted the idea of films as "successful" or "admirable," films that might be "either artistic or commercial" successes. Fulford pointed to several valuable features that had been made but had failed to find an audience, largely because of the CFDC's inaction on distribution and exhibition. (Fulford did not remind his readers that he had trashed one of the most innovative features of the sixties, Paul Almond's *Isabel*, and thereby helped to destroy the filmmaker's career; the directors that he cites all worked in the realist mode.) Fulford's conclusion was the CFDC was now "mired in discredited practices and closely associated with people

FIGURE II

Proudly displaying a vintage car from his prized collection.

who should never have been allowed near public money."

Fulford's diatribe aroused a storm of controversy and a spate of major articles in several newspapers. Producer André Link took issue with Fulford in the pages of *Cinema Canada* in an open letter headed "Delaney's Dreary Denigrations." In separate interviews with Robert Martin and Jamie Portman, both the chair and the executive director of the CFDC defended its policies on the grounds that it had been charged with developing a film industry with the understanding that "it takes all kinds of films to make a film industry." The respected film critic Peter Harcourt sided with Fulford, declaring that "*Shivers* reflects the desperation of total cultural cynicism — a cynicism that believes an indigenous Canadian product is neither possible nor worthwhile." Cronenberg himself said that the idea that Canadians should only make "nice and somewhat serious" films was "the same old bullshit which has produced so many deadly films. Where else but in Canada," he rhetorically asked Stephen Chesley, would you find a critic (Fulford) "more conservative, more reactionary" than the CFDC itself, a critic who quoted a politician "for his definition of art?" Why, he complained in an interview with Robert Hookey, should he be penalized for wanting to work in the horror genre in which he had "a lifetime interest and fascination"?

This debate at times became downright silly, degenerating into discussions of the relative merits of "art" and "commerce," as though they were mutually incompatible. There were even discussions on how one might define the "Canadianness" of a feature film. Cronenberg's contribution to this discussion was both sensible and deceptively simple. "Essentially," he said to Hookey, "my films are Canadian because I'm Canadian — therefore my sensibilities are Canadian." Bizarre as the debate was, it was not without impact in the corridors of political power. The press and MPS asked questions of the secretary of state (whose responsibilities included the CFDC), making the bureaucrats more than somewhat nervous over the publicity. Cronenberg mentioned to Sammon that he was told that for days people

FIGURE 12

Lining up a shot for Scanners.

associated with the secretary of state ran around asking: "What are we going to do about Cronenberg?" The debate sparked by Fulford had given the film, and Cronenberg, more publicity than anyone could have bought. Cronenberg seemed to revel — publicly at least — in his notoriety and cheerfully admitted later that he had deliberately encouraged his "Schlockmeister" and "Baron of Blood" labels. At the same time, the debate made the CFDC somewhat apprehensive; funding was refused for his next script, *Rabid*, and Cinépix only managed to produce the film by cross-financing it with another. And the organizers of the Canadian Film Awards (predecessor of the Genies) refused even to consider it for the competition.

Cronenberg's private life during this period was no more placid than his public one. He and Margaret were divorcing and were shortly to be embroiled in a bitter court battle over custody of their daughter. Margaret joined a Gnostic Christian sect in California; David was living with Carolyn Zeifman in an apartment on Cottingham Street, and they were soon to marry. He told Katherine Govier in 1979 that his first impulse after the separation had been to get married again and have more children. Despite the unusual interrelated nature of the breakup and the new relationship, he said he was "very traditional. Having affairs just isn't enough. I like monogamy. Anything else just isn't obsessive enough for me." Carolyn and David Cronenberg later added a son and another daughter to their family.

In early 1977, Robert Fulford's vitriolic article came home to them in a directly personal way when the owner of their apartment evicted them on the grounds of Fulford's comments. She had read an article in the *Globe and Mail* on the upcoming release of *Rabid*. It quoted extensively from Fulford and noted that the star of the new film was Marilyn Chambers, who had gained fame in pornographic movies. The owner knew Fulford personally and knew that he wouldn't lie. And because she was a member of an antipornographic group, she could not tolerate Cronenberg's presence in her house. In a witty but emotional response in the *Globe and Mail*, Cronenberg wrote:

. . . I realized that I had just tangled with Attila the Hun, the leader of the Mongol hordes of my most paranoid dreams. I had always secretly expected him to come to my door, and now, at last, he had come. . . . The nightmare paranoia of my own films was coming home to haunt me. I was not too rattled to see the wonderful symmetry of it all.

His previous reaction to Fulford's article had been "so cool, so fashionably calm." Now he allowed himself "to fully resent the despicable hysteria of the Fulford piece. . . . How dare he! This man wanted to take away both my livelihood and the expression of my dreams and nightmares — a clean sweep." Cronenberg realized that he was not exempt

from the fabled insecurity of the artist, the seer, the prophet, the Jew, the alien who can live happily in someone else's house or country only until he is . . . recognized. Then it's the knock on the door in the middle of the night. . . .

After briefly considering an appeal to the Human Rights Commission, Cronenberg found a small revenge by buying a house across the street. He and his family needed "a fortress against the ravages of the Hun." Even then he was not left alone. As he described it in his article, a city zoning inspector appeared with an "anonymous" complaint that he was operating a commercial pornographic movie business in a residential area. Cronenberg invited him in: "I felt confident and secure. This man would find nothing. He did not know what to look for."

As for Fulford, he remained unrepentant, saying some years later that he felt no obligation to see any other Cronenberg film.

"YOU SHIVER BECAUSE IT'S GOOD"

It took some months (and, no doubt, the influence of positive reviews in Europe) before critics began to address the film as

FIGURE 13

On the set of Scanners: *a quiet moment*
during a difficult production.

other than well-made trash. Thematic concerns were identified and related to Cronenberg's earlier work: the mind-body link, sexual permissiveness, hedonism, scientists as simultaneously benign and malignant. The character of Emil Hobbes was understood as a descendant of the seventeenth-century philosopher Thomas Hobbes, who had insisted on the primacy of humanity's physical nature over the world of the mind. Critics pointed to the use of signs on the walls of the doctor's office. These included William Blake's "The road of excess leads to the palace of wisdom" (a literary justification of Cronenberg's view that art should be extreme) and "Sex is the invention of a clever venereal disease" (a witty play on Burroughs's "sex is a virus"). Many critics found the film highly moralistic, with the liberating sexuality leading only to a new form of repression. Canadian critic Maurice Yacowar even wondered in "You Shiver Because It's Good" whether attacks on this "traditionally moral work" by critics such as Fulford meant that they were "secret swingers chafing under Cronenberg's lash." Other critics, including Robin Wood, found the film essentially reactionary in its insistence that attempting to change the world only made it profoundly worse. The critical view that Cronenberg's films contain only contagion and death without offering positive alternatives has continued as an influential one in terms of interpreting his work. However, it tends to overlook Cronenberg's own views on "balance" and his sense of apparently contradictory things being inextricably bound together. Liberation and repression are two sides of the same coin. As he put it to Rodley, "The reason I'm secure is because I'm crazy. The reason I'm stable is because I'm nuts. It's palpable to me."

The film's release in the United States was disappointing. Some scenes were cut in order to avoid an American X-rating, print quality was poor, and the distribution badly handled. It was retitled *They Came from Within*, a title as reminiscent of Hollywood fifties horror films as Cronenberg's original but actually more descriptive of the theme than *Shivers*. The film was largely ignored, and Cronenberg did not begin to attract attention in the United States until after the release of *Rabid* a year later.

The reviews in Europe were mostly positive, with French critics being the most enthusiastic. These critics tended to view the film as a quasi-surrealist attack on bourgeois notions of morality and sexuality. This view undoubtedly delighted Cronenberg because it meant that he had captured something of Burroughs's ideas about the bourgeois lifestyle in which he grew up. Burroughs felt that the dullness of bourgeois existence was not harmless but a positive evil growing out of repressed sexuality and the oppression of the lower classes. It is in this context that we can understand Cronenberg's later comment to Beard and Handling that "the ending of *Shivers* was for me a happy ending." Cronenberg continues to have ambivalent feelings about "middle-class normality."

It is possible to consider *Shivers* as a pop pastiche of Burroughs, especially *Naked Lunch*. In the novel, Burroughs has an entity called the "Human Virus" or the "evil virus" living off the human host, satisfying its own needs for drugs, sex, or power. Once possessed by the virus, human beings become dehumanized, subservient to physical or psychological needs, and gradually regress to a lower form of life. Social structures, like individuals, can also be possessed by viruses that warp and control them for their own needs. In *Naked Lunch*, the most significant characters exerting social control are doctors. The parallels with *Shivers* are evident.

In any case, *Shivers* established Cronenberg as the professional filmmaker that he had determined to become. Even before the release of the film, he was offered more television directing at the CBC. He was invited by John Hirsch, a theatre producer and director who had just joined the CBC, to take part in a video training course for young directors. He went on to direct (but not write) two half-hour dramas for the Peep Show series: *The Victim* and *The Lie Chair*. They were shot in August and October 1975 respectively, prior to the release of *Shivers*, but not telecast until early 1976. Cronenberg later wrote and directed another half-hour drama for CBC's Teleplay series: *The Italian Machine*. Shot in April 1976, it is an eccentric and comic story featuring a rare and beautiful motorcycle lusted after by several characters, and it reflects something of Cronenberg's own passion for racing machines. It also gave him more experience working with actors on a film set — including several who were to appear in his later features. Telecast in December 1976, it was his most successful foray into television. It was also to be his last until 1990. He wanted to get back into feature-film production. He had already submitted a treatment to John Dunning of Cinépix for what eventually became *Rabid*. Despite the furore over *Shivers*, Cronenberg continued, as he told Rodley, to have "full confidence that everything I was doing was great."

"I'LL BE THE FIRST CRONENBERG"

Over the next seven years, Cronenberg was to make six more feature films. All but one (*Fast Company*, a film about drag racing) were horror/science-fiction films. *Rabid*, *The Brood*, *Scanners*, *Videodrome*, and *The Dead Zone* collectively form the core of what was increasingly recognized as a kind of Cronenbergian sub-genre structured around forms and themes quite different than in the traditional horror genre. They continued to be marketed as horror films, and that proved to be something of a mixed blessing. Although the genre allowed him considerable freedom to innovate, it did have restrictions and inevitably limited his audience. Cronenberg did not intend to continue forever as a "cult" director. He was reaching for artistic respectability and a wider audience. He had said to Robert Martin in 1976 that he didn't want to become Canada's Roger Corman: "I'll be the first Cronenberg. . . . I have something that has been lacking in Canada, a real artistic vision. They can, and in England they do, talk about a Cronenbergesque film." Although none of his films fits within established generic conventions, *Videodrome* was to be his first clear step away from the horror genre. His films since then resemble nothing in cinema except other Cronenberg films.

At the same time, however, as he moved toward a wider acceptability and respectability, he remained committed to the idea of excess as essential in artistic creation. "One of the reasons people like to see my movies," he said to John Colapinto, "is that they expect that I will go farther than they would. It's part of my relationship with my audience." He delights in telling the story of his friend, filmmaker Peter Rowe, who liked *Videodrome* but told him, "You know, someday they're going to lock you up." Rowe's comment confirmed him as an artistic outsider; his recounting it to Beard and Handling indicates his continuing dedication to the role.

During these years, Cronenberg also established himself in the industry as a consummate professional. He was comfortable working with producers and was not snobbish about the financing side of the industry as something unworthy of his attention. He developed a reputation as a director capable of completing a film on time and within budget. Among actors and technicians he is now known as well organized, calm, and reasonable, a director who truly wants all involved to do their best. As Martha Jones observed him on the set of *Fast Company*, she noted, "Patience, earnestness, and gentleness are words that come to mind." Although actors are not encouraged to improvise or interfere with his script during shooting, he is known among them for his collaborative approach. Acting is for him an important element in filmmaking — he is not like other directors notorious for treating actors with disdain. Before and during shooting, he will sit and discuss their roles with actors so that there is a shared understanding. He values flexibility — to the point where he is prepared to rewrite scenes during shooting. As he told Mark Czarnecki, "A good director has to react to the energy on his set and the energy of the actor." During these years, "professionalism" became his watchword, and his use of the term in relation to collaborators became one of highest praise.

When a film is completed, Cronenberg takes part with equal

gusto in the marketing and promotion that follow. (A famous, though probably apocryphal, example is when he called for "More blood, more blood!" during shooting when a journalist was present.) He now enjoys the artistic freedom to choose projects, and it stems in no small measure from the reputation for professionalism that he developed between the midseventies and the mideighties. As his friend Norman Snider remarked to Czarnecki in 1983, "The film industry is tough — you aren't handed out points for being nice and shy. David knows exactly what he wants and gets it."

In 1976, however, Cronenberg still had a long way to go. If *Shivers* had brought him a certain notoriety, it had not given him much critical recognition. Cinépix had been pleased with *Shivers* and wanted to do another one. Cronenberg gave it an outline of a script called "Mosquito," which he had worked on during the frustrations of trying to produce *Shivers*. It was about a female vampire who develops the affliction after plastic surgery goes wrong. It was on a bigger scale than the isolated setting of *Shivers* and involved rabid maniacs running amok in the streets of Montreal. While writing the script for what became *Rabid* in John Dunning's house near Montreal, Cronenberg began to lose faith in the idea. He wondered whether it wasn't merely ridiculous. He told Rodley that Dunning reassured him that it was "compelling and weird." Perhaps more persuasively, he urged Cronenberg to complete it because time had passed since his first movie, and "You have to keep the momentum going." The possible collapse of his new career before it had hardly begun was enough to sustain Cronenberg's drive.

Rabid went into production in November 1976. Its budget (over $500,000) was still low by industry standards but considerably higher than that for *Shivers*. The CFDC initially refused to invest in the film because of the "official" reaction to *Shivers*; it only did so after Michael Spencer suggested a cross-financing arrangement with another Cinépix project. Cronenberg had originally thought of Sissy Spacek (prior to her fame in *Carrie*) for the leading role. However, producer Ivan Reitman had already

FIGURE 14

A gleeful filmmaker displays his first
Genie Award for Best Director in 1984.

approached one-time porno star, Marilyn Chambers (famous for her role in films such as *Behind the Green Door*), who wanted to move into "legitimate" movies. The commercially astute Reitman knew that her name would help to sell the film to distributors, especially in foreign markets.

Cronenberg's initial impression of her was not favourable. She had been working in Las Vegas, and he thought that she represented a kind of world that was totally foreign to him. Later he realized that she was a dedicated professional who worked hard on the set. He told Lee Rolfe in 1977 that "She was willing to do whatever was necessary to make the film work and didn't complain about the cold and the mud and that kind of thing." Cronenberg also spoke about "the need for professionalism" in filmmaking and noted that he would now find it impossible to go back to "amateurs." Despite Chambers's professional work on *Rabid*, she was never accepted in the "legitimate" industry and returned to making porno movies.

The story of *Rabid* tells of a woman who, following a near-fatal motorcycle accident, undergoes plastic surgery only to find that it has an unexpected side effect. She grows a retractable, phallus-like organ under her armpit and develops an appetite for human blood. In order to stay alive, she must suck human blood with her new appendage, and her attacks cause hundreds of Montrealers to foam at the mouth and run around biting people. The disease is brought under control only when she is bitten by one of her own rabid victims and finally dies. In the original script, but missing from the film, is a ten-second dialogue scene that explains the origin of the bloodsucking organ. In it the surgeon discloses that he had used a new tissue-graft technique that was supposed to grow for her the new intestines that she needed to survive, but the new tissue did something else instead (Emergent Evolutionism again). Cronenberg cut the dialogue because it broke up the pace of the scene, but he later decided that the cut had been a mistake. "I find that people generally just don't get it . . ." he told Lee Rolfe. "It paralleled the premise of *Shivers* as being a kind of absurd, but vaguely possible, scientific achievement. . . ." When Rolfe asked him why he had chosen to put the new organ in the woman's armpit, Cronenberg responded, "Where else would you put it? . . . [T]ry thinking of another place that will work and get you passed [sic] the censors."

More suspenseful in its structure than *Shivers*, the film neatly mixes elements of science fiction and horror and is leavened by a wonderfully bizarre sense of humour that undoubtedly helped its appeal. Its larger budget gave Cronenberg the opportunity to return to something of the visual style and sensibility apparent in his first features. Released in the spring of 1977, it went on to gross some $7 million worldwide. It was particularly successful in Britain, where the fear of a rabies epidemic is almost a national phobia.

Critics were also beginning to notice that there were themes common to both films: contagion, sexuality, the horror of the body rather than the traditional horror of the soul. Canadian critics, however, were no more kind to this film than they had been to *Shivers* — though Joan Irving perceptively noted that "it seems likely that the film was intended to set him up for the kind of projects that will one day carry him beyond the critics' barbs."

After shooting was completed on *Rabid* in late 1976, Cronenberg was not to go behind a camera again for almost two years. The debilitating child-custody battle with his ex-wife was (as he later told Colapinto) "one of the worst things that ever happened to me." His landlady had evicted him, and he had bought a house with the attendant implications of a mortgage. He was supposed to be working on a script called "The Sensitives" (which later became *Scanners*) for producers Pierre David and Victor Solnicki, but another idea kept getting in the way. This was the story for what eventually became *The Brood*. It was to be a script steeped in bitterness, which, Cronenberg later admitted, was written as an act of revenge against his ex-wife.

Apart from his script writing he had no work, and he again had to live through a difficult period. He told Chris Rodley that he could "remember writing *The Brood* with gloves on, because it was unheated upstairs. It was winter, and freezing. I cut the fingers off the gloves so I could type."

Cronenberg also felt quite isolated from his peers in the Canadian film industry, given the kind of films he made and the kind of Canadian films that Canadian critics appeared to prefer. His sense of isolation only lifted when he was invited to the Banff convention of the Motion Picture Institute of Canada in January 1978. He was delighted to meet directors such as Paul Almond, one of the few Canadian filmmakers who also worked in a nonnaturalist mode and who had equally suffered from Canadian critical attacks. *Rabid* was screened as a current example of production in Canada, and for once Cronenberg didn't face rejection. "They reacted to it as *film*," he said to Govier. "I was beseiged [sic] by producers." It also confirmed him in his commitment to commercial, mainstream filmmaking. Some Canadian directors and critics might think that he was successful only because he had compromised his talents for financial gain, but "That's not true": "The fact is that the kind of films I make are the kind of films people like to see." It was through a connection made at the convention that his next film emerged.

Fast Company, a drag-racing film, was shot in July and August 1978 on location near Edmonton. It was the first feature film that Cronenberg directed from a script by someone else and his first film without a horror/science-fiction theme. Its racing theme, however, was by no means remote to him. Since he was an adolescent, Cronenberg has had a passion for racing cars and motorbikes, and he still collects them. At times he has driven a Ferrari or a Porsche. Indeed, producer Michael Lebowitz hired Cronenberg for the film partly because of his knowledge of racing machines.

Although Cronenberg was working from a script created by other hands, he conveyed a deep sense of commitment to everyone on the set. Martha Jones reported on his "sense of caring as he talks about the film, the conscientiousness of his direction," and his air of total concentration when working. When she questioned him about his meticulous attention to detail, she noted an "almost Zen-like" response:

"It can be like a drag race . . . or a long-distance run, or a boxing match . . . anything that requires endurance and total involvement. You have to be focused on exactly what's going on at the moment. Just because it's three in the morning, you don't let up your concentration . . . it'll show in the final work."

Fast Company tells of a sympathetic group of drivers and mechanics who have to struggle against the machinations of their corrupt corporate boss. Apart from characteristic touches of Cronenberg's cool, detached visual style, the film is not particularly memorable. In retrospect, its significance perhaps lies in the fact that it brought together for the first time many people who were to become continuing members of Cronenberg's production team. These included cinematographer Mark Irwin, art director Carol Spier, editor Ronald Sanders, costumer Delphine White, and sound technician Bryan Day. They were later joined by music composer Howard Shore (another friend since high school) and Denise Woodley, Cronenberg's sister.

Fast Company had been financed under a tax-incentive scheme introduced in 1976 and designed to encourage private investment in the film industry. Although well intentioned, it grew into a loophole for evading taxes because investors only had to contribute a small amount of cash (and a promissory note) in order to claim a tax credit for a much larger sum. Until the regulations were changed a few years later, the Canadian film industry went into an annual boom-and-bust cycle. From November to April, production boomed as potential investors with excess income sought a tax shelter; then it floundered for the rest of the year. Many films produced in these years were never released because the tax shelter was more important than the films themselves. Cronenberg articulated his perspective on the period to Rodley, noting that "All the abuses people remember that era for were real." He pointed out that companies such as Cinépix

were movie people. . . . But this was a whole other era of lawyers and brokers suddenly becoming producers overnight because they could raise the money. They knew the tax-shelter laws. . . . People would get their two hundred grand for getting the money together, and didn't care after that. They didn't know enough about the film business to even make the movie successful commercially so they could make more money.

At the time, however, Cronenberg quickly positioned himself to take advantage of this new financing opportunity.

Cronenberg told Rodley that he thought that *Fast Company* had some potential as "a good solid B-movie actioner, as they say." However, as with so many other tax-shelter films, lawyers had the final say. Although officially released in the spring of 1979, the film's American distributor almost immediately went bankrupt and ownership went into litigation. The film had few theatrical screenings, but it is now fairly regularly scheduled on late-night TV — unlike Cronenberg's other films, whose imagery doubtless makes TV programmers nervous.

The experience of *Fast Company* was soon behind Cronenberg. His new script was completed, financing raised (by both the CFDC and tax-shelter investments, for a total of $1.5 million), and the production structure in place. Two months after directing *Fast Company*, Cronenberg was shooting *The Brood*. He would work, for the first time, with two stars: Oliver Reed and Samantha Eggar.

BROODING

Webster's defines *brood* as (1) the young birds from a clutch of eggs or a large family of children; (2) to sit on and hatch eggs; or (3) to think about sullenly, especially after an injury or insult. Cronenberg evidently intended all three meanings, but the last is by far the most potent. He has said many times that the film was autobiographical in origin; however, it "ended up nowhere near autobiography in strict terms," he told Rodley, "because I refuse to have invention taken away from me." He wrote the script during the traumatic period of his divorce and the struggle for custody of his daughter. At one point his ex-wife announced that she was taking Cassandra to a religious community in California; Cronenberg had to get a court order to prevent her from doing so. "And then she left," he told Rodley. "After swearing that she would never leave her daughter, she signed her over to me so that she could go." He thinks of *The Brood* as his version of *Kramer vs Kramer* but truer to the emotional realities involved. "When I saw 'Kramer' I was amazed at how sweet everyone was," he said to Jack Kroll. "It's false and oversimplified — where's the real sense of anger, the anguish over irretrievable loss, where's the urge to kill?"

Cronenberg's alter ego is *The Brood*'s Frank Carveth, a father who tries to get his little girl away from the clutches of a very sick mother who may have abused her daughter and who has decided that she would prefer her daughter dead to being in her father's custody. Ultimately the mother is destroyed. "I can't tell you how satisfying that scene is," Cronenberg told Paul Sammon. "I wanted to strangle my ex-wife."

Personal motivations aside, *The Brood* was to be one of Cronenberg's most inventive and satisfying works. If he had earlier explored the assumed Cartesian separation between mind and body, the theme in *The Brood* is given a sharper focus with the premise that the world of the mind also has real, external manifestations. The story is about Nola Carveth (a woman full of rage against her parents and her estranged husband), who is incarcerated in the Somafree Institute. It is run by Dr. Raglan, the author of *The Shape of Rage* and inventor of Psychoplasmics — a somewhat sinister version of the heightened-awareness and quasi-religious movements then popular in California. Nola expresses her emotional rage physically by giving birth from a transparent uterus on the outside of her body to a brood of vicious little creatures that kill at her command. Both Nola's parents are killed, as is Dr. Raglan, who realizes too late the error of his methods. Frank strangles his wife and escapes with his daughter, but neither notices that she is developing a small welt on her arm.

The film began production in Toronto in mid-November when the Cronenberg's newly acquired home had been stripped to studs and joists for some time, awaiting renovation. Cronenberg joked at the time that he made the character in the film a house renovator in the hope of getting the place fixed up during production. As Govier noted, he was not so lucky — though he was able to complete the renovations when the film was finished. Some scenes were shot at Brown's School, where Cassandra was a pupil. The film also featured eight young gymnasts from Mississauga, Ontario, as the grotesque brood. As Diane Francis reported from the set, the youngsters had to undergo three-hour makeup sessions involving the gluing of membrane masks to their faces. "They wore blue and yellow cotton pajamas with humps sewn inside the backs. The whole hideous look was topped off with white fright wigs." The kids performed with skill and apparent relish in scenes that terrified watching parents.

Cronenberg was delighted to have the accomplished Oliver Reed for the central role of Dr. Hal Raglan. He told Noah James that Reed had accepted less than his usual fee "because he said it was the best script he'd been offered since *The Devils*." Reed would later insist that *The Brood* was the most frightening film in which he had appeared. Samantha Eggar worked for only three days on the set in a role that required her never to move from a sitting or kneeling position. Although she had earlier told Cronenberg that the script had echoes of her own childhood, she later described it as the most repulsive film on which she had ever worked.

Also joining the Cronenberg team for the first time was music composer Howard Shore. He had played flute and saxophone for Lighthouse in the sixties and was then music director for *Saturday Night Live* in New York. He, too, accepted a smaller-than-usual fee because he wanted to work with the man whom he considered a major artist. "Of all the people I knew," he told Katherine Govier, "David had the most vision of what he wanted to do. Twelve years ago he was into the seeds of what he's making now."

The Brood was Cronenberg's most accomplished film to date. It has a nicely sustained tone of melancholy, though some critics missed the leavening of black humour of the earlier films. Working with a decent budget, a professional team of actors, and excellent technical resources, Cronenberg created a terrifying vision of the scars that parents impose on their children. While the premise of hostility given physical form is simple, it is also powerful. And Cronenberg's expression of the theme is far from simple. His cool, unhysterical style was perfect for showing a commonplace world of normal surfaces hiding ugly and unacknowledged passions.

Cronenberg was also beginning to be noticed by more receptive journalists. Earlier, long-time friend John Hofsess had written an article for the *Canadian* magazine extolling Cronenberg's "exciting, and profitable," approach rather than drearily searching for "The Great Canadian Movie." Now, in time for the release of *The Brood*, both *Maclean's* and *Toronto Life* published largely sympathetic profiles.

The film, however, did not fare well in distribution, being sold in the United States as a typical, exploitation B-movie. Marketing practices for horror films were already beginning to work against Cronenberg's quest for a broader audience.

SCANNING

The problem with movies about telepathy has always been how to make it physical. And I do mean *physical*, since for me it's never enough just to make something visual.

— *Cronenberg to David Chute in 1980*

The demands of tax-shelter financing led Cronenberg to move almost immediately into his next film. His producers, Pierre

David and Victor Solnicki, already had the financing, but principal photography had to be completed before the end of December 1979 in order to meet tax-shelter requirements. Cronenberg returned to the earlier drafts of "The Sensitives," a story about telepathy that echoed some of the themes of *Stereo*.

Although Cronenberg had his biggest budget to date ($4.1 million), he only had three weeks to complete the script. The result was that it was being constantly rewritten during production. Sometimes Cronenberg had to write or revise the script for the day's shooting between five and seven in the morning — in a building in Montreal without heating or insulation. There were also, Cronenberg told Sammon, "Times when everyone went to lunch and I wrote the scene that was coming up. Naturally, the actors were very insecure about all this, as well they should be." When actress Jennifer O'Neill arrived, she was disturbed to discover not only that the name of her character had been changed but also that she had been sent a script (by the producers, without Cronenberg's knowledge) from which all the violence had been excised. As Cronenberg told Rodley, "When she saw the real script, she started to sob and cry in the trailer and was really disturbed and upset and didn't want to be a part of this movie." It took all of Cronenberg's well-known calm and patience to persuade her to continue.

Patrick McGoohan, playing the role of Dr. Ruth, the sinister head of Consec, proved even more difficult. Although Cronenberg was later to praise McGoohan's acting and screen presence, it is obvious that, for once, he had to deal with an actor who resisted the collaborative approach on set that he had so carefully developed. Cronenberg found him constantly angry as well as self-destructive. He told Paul Sammon that, because of last-minute script changes, McGoohan was always ranting and raving that "he didn't understand what was going on." Not surprisingly, he and Cronenberg parted after the film on not particularly good terms — one of Cronenberg's few failures in his relationships with actors.

The first day of shooting was an augury of the difficulties to follow. Cronenberg described it to Rodley as "the most disastrous shooting day I've ever had." He continued:

> We went out, and there was nothing to shoot. Nothing was there: we didn't have the truck; we didn't have the insignia on the building; we didn't have the costume for Stephen Lack. We were shooting along the expressway, and the traffic was jamming up. A guy in a truck was watching us shooting by the side of the road and didn't notice that everyone in front of him had stopped. I turned round in time to see his truck climb up on top of this little Toyota. Our grips had to jump the fence and drag these two women out of their car and lay them on the verge. Dead. It was hideous. Everybody was just shocked and depressed. We weren't responsible, but if we hadn't been there, it wouldn't have happened. It was just a total wipe-out. All because we had to start shooting.

The problems continued even after the principal scenes with the actors had been finished. Second-unit photography was not completed (technically illegal under tax-shelter regulations) until early 1980. As Cronenberg noted to Rodley, the tax-shelter era put "abnormal time pressures on everybody, not just the director, to do weird stuff to get it to happen in time." The famous exploding-head scene was created by Chris Walas, who later worked with Cronenberg on the fly effects of *The Fly* and the creatures of *Naked Lunch*.

Time pressures also generated several structural flaws in the film and an ending that did not work. Cronenberg prevailed on his producers to allow him to shoot three additional scenes and also to reshoot the ending involving the telepathic duel between the two brothers. Despite these changes, there remain some puzzling gaps in the plot that are not of the same order as the ambiguities in Cronenberg's other films. As a result of the changes, the film was not released until early 1981, an unusually long time for postproduction. Test screenings led to other changes, including a move of the exploding-head scene to later in the film. Although Cronenberg initially resisted having to hold test screenings, he later came to value the practice and now uses them for all his films.

The pressures of the production schedule no doubt also helped to shape a film that is less personal than Cronenberg's others. Although there are a few of his personal themes, *Scanners* is as close to a standard action thriller with a science-fiction plot as Cronenberg has ever come, with an emphasis on linear action, mystery, suspense, and chases. The film's premise is that a scientist had developed a tranquillizer drug called Ephemerol for pregnant women that causes their children to be born with telepathic powers. Years later, these children have grown to be "good" and "bad" scanners involved in a struggle for control with Dr. Paul Ruth, the drug's inventor and head of the mysterious Consec. The action sequences are relatively routine, at least for Cronenberg, and, apart from the exploding head and the final duel, there is little body horror and no reference to sexuality. It stands in total contrast to the personally obsessed *The Brood*. As Cronenberg remarked humorously to Sammon at the time, "I've remarried. I have another kid, and I'm feeling much more optimistic about things in general. Now that I'm feeling so good, I'm exploding heads just like any other young, normal North American boy." Cronenberg was still prepared in the early eighties to continue exploiting his reputation as the "Baron of Blood." But he was soon to find this reputation more onerous than helpful as he began to move away from the horror genre.

Scanners, however, was the film that introduced a wider audience to Cronenberg's work. *The Brood* had been marketed in the United States as a B-horror movie, so Cronenberg's producers decided to deal with another distributor that could market *Scanners* more broadly. Their decision was a success. *Scanners* was widely reviewed in the mainstream media. Its box-office receipts in its first week shot it into the top position on the *Variety* chart of gross receipts. Kroll noted in *Newsweek* that the film "climaxes [Cronenberg's] five-year rise to the top of the horror heap." The film's success also led to his being noticed by Hollywood. He was offered the chance to direct a sequel but refused — and received neither credit for the original idea nor royalties.

Partly to capitalize on the favourable publicity, Cronenberg's producers announced in a full-page ad in *Variety* that his next project would be "David Cronenberg's Frankenstein." Cronenberg remembers it as little more than a passing idea. When told of it by Pierre David, he had responded: "Sounds good to me. What about poor Mary Shelley?" If he were to do it, he said to Sammon, ". . . I'd try to retain Shelley's original concept of the creature being an intelligent, sensitive *man*. Not just a beast."

Cronenberg's next project, however, was also determined under the pressures of tax-shelter financing. When asked by producer Pierre David for ideas, Cronenberg offered two, of which David chose the one that eventually became *Videodrome*. It started out as a conspiracy thriller, similar to *Scanners*, that was called "Network of Blood." Later, Cronenberg told Tim Lucas, he developed the notion of a first-person narrative that would subjectively show the course of a person's insanity. "Our own perception of reality is the only one we'll accept, it's all we have to go on and, if you're going mad, that is still your reality. But," he added, "the same thing, seen from an outside perspective, is a person acting insane." As he started to write the script, however, his ideas and imagery became increasingly bold and bizarre. He was sure, he told Rodley, that the producers would reject his first draft because "It was so much more extreme than my premise had suggested." To Cronenberg's surprise they liked it, though doubting that it could be filmed as he had written it. In the event, several of the scenes were never filmed, and others that were shot were excised in the editing room. One scene never filmed would have been a brief extension of the ending beyond the central character's suicide. Cinematographer Mark Irwin outlined the scene to Tim Lucas:

> "He'll shoot himself in the head and go — boom! — out of the frame, and we'll cut to his head hitting the clay wall, and the camera will track back and there he is, happy in front of

the fireplace with his pipe and slippers and Nicki hopping all over him! Another film for the whole family!"

An entire special-effects sequence was also abandoned late in the production after tests persuaded Cronenberg that the sequence could not be shot to his standards.

With *Videodrome*, Cronenberg moved further away from the conventions of horror and science fiction. Conceptually more complex than his earlier work, it would explore some of his characteristic themes with a new maturity and authority and extend his range into new ones — such as the ideas of Canadian media philosopher Marshall McLuhan. Mark Czarnecki noted that *Videodrome* was like a Burroughsian interpretation of McLuhan's influential book, *Understanding Media: The Extensions of Man*. In the film, Cronenberg was also to confront the censorious impulses of some critics concerning the sexual and violent imagery in his work. "I wanted," he told Rodley, "to see what it would be like, in fact, if what the censors were saying would happen, did happen. What would it feel like? What would it lead to?"

VIEWING

Videodrome went into production in Toronto in late October 1981. Absent were the pressures that had marred the production experience of *Scanners*, even considering that Cronenberg was working with an inexperienced actress, rock star Deborah Harry. James Woods, in the lead role, was the consummate professional. John McKinnon reported from the set that he was "remarkably relaxed, typically sardonic. Someone asks him if he's on his mark. Woods replies that he tapes his mark to his shoe. 'That way I never go wrong.' " Cronenberg told Rodley that the actor's "presence on the screen began to feel like a projection of me. It was exciting to find an actor who was my

FIGURE 15

On the set of Videodrome *with his son.*

cinematic equal. . . . It was nice to hear Jimmy do dialogue that I had written."

However, despite the better conditions, there were still delays and difficulties — not the least of which was an outbreak of stomach flu among the cast and crew. Given that the film deals with sadomasochism, violence, and torture, it is hardly surprising that some members of the crew became openly disturbed during the production — even though many had often worked with Cronenberg. One of the extras, who insisted on hanging around the set after her (fake) torture scene, did not improve the mood. The script again evolved during shooting, and changes were even made at the postproduction stage. Some dialogue scenes explaining or contextualizing the protagonist's hallucinations were eliminated, and the film is considerably more ambiguous in structure than originally written. Because of the stream of script alterations, and the often short notice of location changes, Cronenberg had to keep reassuring the crew that he still had the film under control.

In its final form, *Videodrome* (comparable to the later *Naked Lunch*) seamlessly fuses two different stories. One is a conspiracy thriller in which Max Renn, owner of Toronto's CIVIC-TV, during his search for sensational programming, discovers a satellite channel broadcasting hard-core sex and violence footage. Determined to track down its source, he is told that it is in Malaysia, only to learn later that it is in Pittsburgh and is being used as part of an international conspiracy to control people's minds. The other story is a first-person narrative following Renn's hallucinations as he increasingly falls prey to the Videodrome signal. In these sequences, the audience sees only what Renn experiences, with no external context by which to measure whether this is "reality" or "hallucination." In fact, Cronenberg insists that there is no difference. "I was trying to make a film that was as complex as the way I experience reality," he told William Beard and Piers Handling. "I think it's very ambiguous. . . . But I wanted it to be like that because to me that's the truth." He also told David Chute in 1983: "I wanted to create a new *reality*, which is very different from creating another *world*, in the future or on another planet. This is a new reality that has elements of the old, familiar reality woven in — because even a psychotic retains *some* connection with the old world."

The film also includes familiar Cronenbergian themes: psychic states "made flesh"; Emergent Evolutionism and its cautionary reminder that human evolution may not always take benign directions; and the absent professor-scientist who appears to have initiated events without understanding the consequences. In this case it is Professor Brian O'Blivion, apparently a dead media guru who has recorded his theories on videotape. The central character, Max Renn, is something of an alter ego for Cronenberg: his portrait displays a remarkable self-awareness, not least in the character's addiction to extreme images and his often self-serving justifications. Cronenberg hinted at the parallels to Rodley when he discussed "Max's take on life," which he was not sure that

> everybody gets. . . . He hasn't reached a point in his life where he actually connects with melancholia. But I think it's there — down the line. . . . The essence of him was that he is glib but is being forced to come to terms with some strange, difficult stuff that he's not prepared to deal with in a real way, a real emotional way.

There can be little doubt that Cronenberg is referring both to his earlier self and to his earlier work. And his later films demonstrate that he was coming to terms with his own melancholia.

During preparations for *Videodrome*, producer Pierre David had been making overtures in Hollywood and eventually secured financing from Universal Studios, which became the film's distributor. The initial test screening in Boston, using a remarkably short seventy-five-minute version, was a disaster, and Cronenberg feared that Universal would pull out of the distribution deal. He got the chance to recut, making changes in the structure to try to clarify the narrative. Some eliminations were also required by the Motion Picture Association of America

(MPAA) in order for the film to gain a "Restricted" certificate rather than an "X" rating. Cronenberg agreed to these changes but was later outraged when Universal made additional eliminations without his knowledge or approval. He was, and remains, an outspoken opponent of censorship. In a typically astringent comment, he told Chris Rodley: "Censors tend to do what only psychotics do: they confuse reality with illusion." In arguing that reality should not be confused with the imaginative creation of fiction, Cronenberg's views parallel those of William Burroughs. Burroughs has argued that factual news reports in the press or on television are far more likely to provoke imitation than fiction.

Videodrome was released early in 1983, and the reviews were almost uniformly favourable: even critics who disliked it saw it as a maturation of Cronenberg's earlier work. Some even suggested that it would reach a wider audience, given what Carrie Rickey called its "Orwellian 1984 blueprint" of a video future manipulated by media totalitarians. Unfortunately, the film died at the box office, taking in barely half of what *Shivers* had grossed. Fans of Cronenberg's earlier films were dissatisfied with it, and the potential for a more sophisticated audience open to the film's ideas never materialized. Universal's marketing strategy was at least partly to blame. Cronenberg pointed out to Rodley that "*Videodrome* wasn't an exploitation sell [like *Scanners*] and it wasn't an art sell. I don't know what it was." Given his conviction that it was his most powerful and ambitious film to date, Cronenberg was "devastated":

It's almost like how do you deal with the inevitability of death. If death is inevitable, it means that everything that comes before is irrelevant and trivial and meaningless. . . . Burroughs talks about how writing is dangerous. I know exactly what he means. So, you go on.

Cronenberg might also have agreed with George Orwell's observation that success and virtue are not necessarily the same

FIGURE 16

Shooting The Dead Zone: *cinematographer Mark Irwin is behind the camera.*

thing. The blow to his pride and sense of achievement was somewhat lessened by the fact that he was already shooting his next film, *The Dead Zone,* by the time that he heard news of the film's poor box-office performance.

The Dead Zone, based on a novel by Stephen King, was to be Cronenberg's most naturalistic and palatable film for a mainstream audience, and it did moderately better at the box office than *Videodrome.* Although the film deals with one of Cronenberg's themes, telepathy, and though he helped to shape the way that this is depicted, it is far from a characteristic Cronenbergian film. It is best regarded as a typical Hollywood studio film, professionally and expertly directed by Cronenberg, especially in terms of the acting. He says that he took it on because he felt drained after the passions of *Videodrome* and, as he had with *Stereo* and *Crimes of the Future,* sensed that he had taken an idea as far as he could. "At that point I needed to do something based on somebody else's work, as relief," he explained to Rodley. "I was not ready to write another script." As a project, it developed out of Hollywood contacts that Cronenberg had established in the early eighties through his Hollywood agent, Mike Marcus.

The Dead Zone was a venture by producer Dino De Laurentiis. It was shot in Toronto and southern Ontario in early 1983 and released later the same year. Although the critical reception was warm, box-office receipts were modest. Cronenberg would spend most of the next two years in and around Hollywood, trying to develop new projects. His Hollywood contacts would lead to numerous offers to direct films such as *Witness, Top Gun, Beverly Hills Cop,* and *Total Recall.* Some offers he refused outright; others failed to develop into anything, though the *Total Recall* project took a year (and twelve draft scripts) out of his life before he and the producer, De Laurentiis, finally parted company after failing to agree on a script.

At the same time, the serious critical attention paid to *Videodrome* and *The Dead Zone* brought to a head a controversy that had followed Cronenberg's work from the beginning. This controversy was over his depiction of sexual difference, his tendency to show woman as "other," and, in particular, the numerous scenes involving the humiliation, usually sexual, of women. *Videodrome* especially was accused of being almost brazenly misogynistic. Over the years, Cronenberg has offered a variety of justifications and rationales. His somewhat facile response in the seventies was that he was accused of showing women as sexually passive in one film and in the next as sexually aggressive. More reasonably, he would later claim that his female characters were meant to be specific to the fiction, neither a reflection of women in general nor a reinforcing of stereotypes. And he said to Rodley that he welcomed (and was pleased by) the feminist debates because the horror genre's themes of death and sexuality placed them "automatically in the arena that has become the feminist arena." Cronenberg continues to insist that his work is sexual, not sexist, concerned more with "omni-sexuality" (the term that he used in *Stereo*) than simply with bisexuality. As he explained to David Breskin in 1992, "And to the extent that I'm interested in exploring stuff that's beyond taboo, I would explore . . . any kind of sexuality." To Beard and Handling he has defended his vision as necessarily conditioned by "the fact that I am male, and my fantasies and my unconscious are male. . . . Let [other] people make their own movies — leave me alone to make mine."

There is a certain disingenuous quality to his comments because they do not address a central issue. This is his view — shared with William Burroughs — that there are innate, biologically determined differences between men and women. Cronenberg has spoken of this issue since the birth of his first daughter, claiming to Govier, as a matter of mere empirical observation, that "Women's sensibility is more introspective. A male child is always thinking 'out.'" He would later cite William Burroughs to Chris Rodley in defence of the argument that social conditioning hardly influences sexual difference. "William Burroughs doesn't just say that men and women are different species, he says they're different species with different wills and purposes."

The notion of biologically determined sexual difference is by no means unique to Cronenberg. It is, indeed, one side of a long-standing debate over whether "nature" or "nurture" is the more significant factor in determining sexual difference. Cronenberg continues to hold firmly to the nature side of the debate. This, in some measure, is an explanation — if not a justification — of the way in which he depicted female characters, especially in his early films.

Cronenberg was, in any case, by the time of *Videodrome*, already beginning to turn away from his early visions: away, we might say, from masculine nightmares involving a threatening woman as "other." As his self-awareness in creating the character of Max Renn makes clear, he was beginning to connect with his own melancholia. From *The Fly* on, he would have the confidence to explore this melancholia in his own, self-aware, masculinist terms, without the need for a nightmare "other" to blame.

"BLACK SUN OF MELANCHOLY"

I am the darkly shaded, the bereaved, the inconsolate,
The prince of Aquitaine, with the blasted tower.
My only *star* is dead, and my star-strewn lute
Carries on it the black *sun* of *melancholy.*

— *Gérard de Nerval, "El Desdichado"*

Since the beginning of his career David Cronenberg has thought of himself as an artist whose medium happened to be film rather than as a filmmaker who happened to make art. His early passion had been to create, and he found film almost fortuitously — even though he quickly discovered that it perfectly suited his temperament. He has continued to insist on this image of artist rather than filmmaker. For example, in explaining to David Breskin why he focused on the theme of writing in his version of *Naked Lunch*, he said:

In a way, in coming to grips with writing, with being creative, I think I'm coming *closer* to the basics. And coming closer to the flame by dealing directly with it. Because what is writing but trying to order reality? Trying to make order out of chaos?

Cronenberg echoed this theme in an interview with Chris Rodley when he said:

> But I think on a very straightforward level it's true that any artist is trying to take control of life by organizing it and shaping it and recreating it. Because he knows very well that the real version of life is beyond his control. It's one of the main reasons people create: to have some control over the universe. To me, that's when a movie becomes part of the process of life. . . .

While Cronenberg told Rodley that he does not consider himself "a big fan of the therapy theory of art," his statement precisely reflects some modern psychoanalytical theories of art criticism. These theories, notably those of Julia Kristeva, argue that artists tend to inhabit the melancholic pole of the psychical spectrum. However, unlike psychotics or medically diagnosed melancholiacs, artists have control over the symbolic representations of melancholia. The artwork then becomes the site of a "vanquished" depression. Although melancholia is marked by sadness, this is not nihilistic despair but the equivalent of mourning for a loss: the sadness of separation, captured by Nerval in his metaphor of a "black *sun*." The artist, who has a sense of detachment denied the psychotic, can symbolically represent this sadness and anguish in evoking premonitions of the scissions between life and death and decay, between meaning and non-meaning.

From this perspective, Cronenberg's work can be thought of as a symbolic wrestling with his own sense of melancholy. This view does not imply that his life is represented in his work. Quite the reverse: it implies that his work has been *part* of his life. That he is aware of this relationship is clear in his comment that "a movie becomes part of the process of life" as well as in his statement to Rodley that his later works are autobiographical in the sense that they come from "deep within my nervous system." Cronenberg has also been aware, since his early films, that death is at the centre of his work (though he tended at first to use this fact to explain his working in the horror genre). Recently he has been more explicit about how this element relates to melancholia. In rejecting the view that *The Fly* was a metaphor for AIDS, he said:

I see it as talking about mortality, about our vulnerability, and the tragedy of human loss. The difficulty in accepting it, and the difficulty of coming to terms with it when you've got it. . . . We've all got the disease — the disease of being finite. And consciousness is the original sin: consciousness of the inevitability of our death.

He had been trying in his films, he also told Rodley, to "discover the connection between the physical and the spiritual. . . . It's still a conundrum that drives me mad: the old Bertrand Russell riddle. What's mind? No matter. What's matter? Never mind." This paradox of mind and body is also the paradox of self and other, human and nonhuman, nature and culture. It is also, not least, the paradox of sexual difference. Cronenberg was now to turn toward exploring this difference in terms that he had tentatively broached in *Videodrome*: masculinity and the male unconscious.

As Cronenberg's understanding of his work matured, he came to realize that his male characters were "all really repressed guys." Although they might be a projection of a part of himself that was repressed or undiscovered, he told David Breskin, they were not "my model of ideal behavior." At the same time, "my vision of masculinity as revealed in the movies is not at all the sort of macho-insensitive-rapist that all those feminist critiques present." His next three films, *The Fly*, *Dead Ringers*, and *Naked Lunch*, were to expose male dreams, nightmares, fears, and desires with an emotionally powerful precision. What critic Pam Cook wrote about *Dead Ringers* might well apply to all three: "Its disturbing impact derives from a laying bare of male fantasies in such a way that masculinity itself is revealed as fragile, unstable, even impossible." Just as Max Renn's control of power collapses in *Videodrome*, so the heroes of these films quite literally disintegrate as chaos overtakes their attempts at order. Two of the films end in self-willed deaths, as does *Videodrome*.

These films brought Cronenberg worldwide fame. *The Fly* attracted the attention of mainstream audiences that had ignored his earlier films; its box-office receipts exceeded any of his other films. With *Videodrome* he won his first Genie Award for Best Director. He went on to win an unprecedented two more Best Director Genies — which must have felt like no small revenge after *Shivers* had been barred from even competing. Retrospectives honouring his films were mounted in major cities. And, in 1990, he was named to France's prestigious Chevalier de l'ordre des arts et des lettres. The first book studying his work, edited by Piers Handling, had appeared in 1983. Two more were published in 1992, one a critical study in French by Serge Grunberg, the other a compilation of interviews in English by Chris Rodley.

The three films also represented a definitive break for Cronenberg from the influence of William Burroughs. Although there is a lingering sense of shared concerns, it is difficult to imagine Burroughs creating the profound human anguish and pain of *The Fly* or the struggle to define self and other in *Dead Ringers*. Even *Naked Lunch*, though it retains the quest and stream-of-consciousness structure of the novel, is a film that emphasizes the process of artistic creativity over Burroughs's other themes of control and addiction.

One concern that Cronenberg continued to share with Burroughs was a profound suspicion of the American dream: its materialistic drives, its faith in technology, its belief in a constantly advancing society and the perfectibility of humanity. It is a suspicion shared by many well-known American writers, including Nathaniel Hawthorne, Edgar Allan Poe, and Henry Miller — the title of whose nonfiction book, *The Air-Conditioned Nightmare*, neatly encapsulates a sceptical view of the American project. Cronenberg has always thought that, as a Canadian, he was ideally placed to examine its vices and virtues. To David Breskin he described his feelings about the American dream as "definitely a love-hate relationship." He feels both attracted to American ideals of individualism and repelled by their consequences. As he told John Colapinto, "I'm enough of a Canadian that I don't like chaos." He also thinks that his Canadian background helps to explain why the chaos that overtakes order in his films is more personal than social. To Beard and Handling he described it in these terms: "you have these little pockets of private and personal chaos brewing in the interstices in the structure of general society, which likes to stress its order and control."

American critics have occasionally wondered why Cronenberg has persisted in shooting in Canada when Hollywood has so often beckoned him. He thinks that he does so not only because his "sensibility is Canadian, whatever that is," but also because it gives his films a certain tone and feel. He told Anne Billson the story of

a man who called me up from Santiago, and he said: "The fact that you make your films in Canada makes them even more eerie and dreamlike, because it's like America, but it's not. The streets look American, but they're not, and the accents are American, but not quite. Everything's a little off-kilter; it's sort of like a dream image of America." There's a certain sense of rhythm that I have, and a sense of isolation, that I don't think are very American.

We might add to this a sense of architecture and space, of staging a scene, that "are American, but not quite." Since the beginning of his career, Cronenberg has developed a visual dialectic between his characters and the space and architecture they occupy. Clearly apparent in the Brutalist architecture of *Stereo* or in the sterility of the apartment building in *Shivers*, this trait has gradually become subtler and richer. It is impossible to imagine *The Fly* without the metaphoric parallels between the telepod and the architecture of the old warehouse in which the scientist works. And while it is a common characteristic of American filmmakers to use an exterior long shot to identify a change of locale, Cronenberg's usage is different. He insists on drawing our attention to these *places*, encouraging us to see a relationship between the disjunctive characters and the deadness of the architecture in which they live and work.

In a similar way, Cronenberg often locates scenes in stairwells and corridors. Curator Louise Dompierre has identified these scenes as representing a sense of duality (up and down / coming and going): these locations are therefore ideal sites for depicting dramatic and psychic conflicts. She also considers them as links between other architectural spaces, and they thus convey a sense of being "in between." We could also say that they represent Cronenberg's own sense of being "in between," even his feeling of being an outsider. His Canadian ambivalence, what he has called the "Canadian curse" of being able to "see all sides to the story at once," has necessarily structured the ambiguity underlying his exploration of the dark side of the American dream.

A FATAL OBSESSION: *THE FLY*

As Cronenberg completed *The Dead Zone* in 1983, his international fame still lay in the future. Before the success of *The Fly*, his professional career went through yet another hiatus, marked by stalled projects and a cameo acting appearance in a Hollywood film.

Cronenberg's first project was a comedy script, "Six Legs," which Universal Pictures rejected after seeing the first draft.

FIGURE 17

*Directing Jeff Goldblum how to react during
a transformation scene in* The Fly.

Producer Dino De Laurentiis tried to involve him in a Stephen King follow-up to *The Dead Zone*. He turned down *Star Trek II: The Wrath of Khan* because it would have meant shooting exactly the script as written. He was also offered the opportunity to direct films such as *Flashdance*, *Witness*, *Top Gun*, and *Beverly Hills Cop*. Most of the scripts he found too mainstream, he told Rodley, in the sense that "by page three I know everything. . . . A mainstream movie . . . isn't going to rattle too many cages. . . ." He developed a television series, *Crimes against Nature*, but even the Home Box Office cable network rejected it as too bizarre. (It has since been revised to be filmed in Toronto.)

The only script that Cronenberg came close to filming was *Total Recall* for Dino De Laurentiis. It had been around for some years without finding a workable mix of writers, director, and producer. After a year of working on drafts of the script, including time spent in the producer's Rome studios, Cronenberg put his foot down and insisted that the twelfth draft was as far as he could go. Because De Laurentiis wanted to return to an earlier version, they agreed to part company, amicably, and were later to work together again, briefly, on *Dead Ringers*. It was another five years before *Total Recall* was filmed by director Paul Verhoeven.

With the collapse of the project, Cronenberg told Rodley, he found himself "in dire straits financially. I was just hoping that somehow something would happen that would be honourable, a movie that I could really be happy doing." The closest he came to a film set was when he played a cameo role in *Into the Night*, directed by his friend John Landis. It was on this set that he met Jeff Goldblum, whom he later brought in to star in *The Fly*. Colapinto reported that Cronenberg told a journalist at this time, "I feel like the ghost of the director I once was."

It was not until March 1985 that Cronenberg materialized back into a director. In a surprising turn of fortune that has often marked his career, he was offered the script of *The Fly* by producer and comedian Mel Brooks. Earlier he had been shown the script by his friend, Toronto producer Marc Boyman (later coproducer of *Dead Ringers*), but was then involved in the abortive *Total Recall* project and could not consider it. When he read it again, he realized how certain elements almost eerily reflected his own sensibility. "It was very body-orientated," he told Rodley, "very body-conscious." However, Cronenberg did not intend to engage again in a year of arguing over draft scripts. He told Brooks and producer Stuart Cornfeld that he wanted the freedom to adapt the script, and he was delighted when they accepted. *The Fly* would be shot in the Kleinburg Studios north of Toronto on a budget of approximately $10 million. When released in the summer of 1986, it would gross an astonishing $100 million at the box office.

The original script was, in part, a remake of a modestly effective 1958 horror film, itself based on a rather vapid short story about a scientist who exchanges body parts with a fly. Cronenberg felt that scriptwriter Charles Pogue had rethought and understood the original premise, but, he told Rodley, "the characters were awful, the dialogue trite and the ending bad." Cronenberg set about rewriting the script — and eventually earned an official screenwriting credit from the Writers Guild.

When production got under way in Toronto, all the familiar members of the Cronenberg team were on hand. Producer Stuart Cornfeld from Los Angeles found himself somewhat isolated among a group of Canadians used to working together and became resentful. In the last few crucial weeks of shooting, Colapinto reported from the set, Cornfeld looked "old beyond his thirty-three years, developed dark circles under his eyes and complained of homesickness for Los Angeles." Meanwhile, "Cast, crew, and technicians had long since ceased to pun about 'flies in the ointment.'" Yet, through it all, Cronenberg "showed not the least external sign of pressure" — even though he had had to combat a bout of stomach flu in the first week of shooting and a consequent delay in the schedule.

Jeff Goldblum was cast for the lead role of scientist Seth Brundle. Cronenberg had wanted him for what he described to Rodley as his "very particular and eccentric screen presence," which he had seen on *Into the Night*. Various actresses were considered for the role of the reporter, who becomes Brundle's first lover. Cronenberg eventually succeeded in persuading his producer to hire Geena Davis and thus match real-life romance with on-screen romance. Cronenberg told Rodley that he found Davis "funny and sexy, and to me that is just the most diabolical combination." He later concluded that the off-set relationship between Davis and Goldblum had both advantages and disadvantages in terms of their working together.

The film also had the most spectacular sets and special effects of Cronenberg's career. The transformation (designed by Chris Walas) involved using a mould from a Goldblum body cast to develop a series of costumes as well as puppets that allowed for a metamorphosis in seven stages. The design of the teleportation pod was inspired by the cylinder head and barrel of Cronenberg's Ducati motorcycle. The sets — designed mostly by art director Carol Spier — included the scientist's minutely detailed laboratory and loft and a room capable of rotating 360° within a few seconds. The elaborate sets and effects were persuasive evidence of how far Cronenberg had travelled since his first features.

The biggest crisis of the production came when Mark Irwin, the cinematographer of Cronenberg's previous five films, was called away for personal reasons. A substitute was found, but shooting was delayed an extra two weeks. At this moment of crisis, Cronenberg was also informed that executive producer Mel Brooks had decided to fly up from Los Angeles to check on how the production was going. Although Brooks's inopportune visit created high tension on the set, it turned out to be friendly enough. Colapinto reported that Brooks joked with the technicians and reporters who were standing around, watched a bit of the filming, embraced the director, and left. Throughout, Cronenberg remained calm. He told Colapinto that his model was "Captain Horatio Hornblower when he's standing on the bridge. He knows the Spanish Armada's on his tail, his provisions are down, and he hasn't heard from his admiralty. He doesn't know what the hell to do — and he cannot let anyone know. He

FIGURE 18

David Cronenberg in 1985 on the set of The Fly.

has to exude total confidence." Colapinto noted, almost with a sense of wonder, how serene Cronenberg remained throughout the production. He was, however, not without feelings. Once, directing Goldblum in a particularly harrowing transformation scene, Cronenberg's hands twisted into empathetic claws.

Cronenberg made a cameo appearance in the film as a doctor in a hospital sequence. Jay Scott quotes him in "Director Gets to the Heart" as saying that it was inspired by a comment from director Martin Scorsese. "People are surprised, when they meet me, that I look so normal. Marty said I look like a Beverly Hills gynecologist." (Acting appearances by Cronenberg have become something of a minor specialty. He has starred in a short film, Blue, and a feature, Nightbreed, and he has made cameo appearances not only in The Fly but also in Into the Night, Trial by Jury, and the television series Maniac Mansion. These appearances have not always been amicable. Toronto gossip has it that he was very temperamental and demanding during production of Blue, directed by Don McKellar.)

In Cronenberg's adaptation of Charles Pogue's script, all the characters were changed and only one line of dialogue was retained. What remained of the original, "ironically enough," Cronenberg told Scott, "was the transformation, which was very much me." Pogue's scientist and wife, a couple afflicted by disaster, were rejected as too normal. Cronenberg felt that their normalcy was a weakness that threatened to turn the film into a "disease-of-the-week" TV movie. The scientist evolved into the eccentric Seth Brundle, the wife into a recently met woman who would become his first lover. Even Brundle's fusion with a fly during a teleportation experiment takes place more at the genetic level than at the simple level of transpositioning the fly's head and claw to the scientist in the original. Acting like a virus or cancer, in the manner of Emergent Evolution, the fusion slowly transforms Brundle into something that had never existed. He is neither fly nor man but "Brundlefly." It was, for Cronenberg, a metaphor for disease and aging: How does the man deal with his disease? How does his lover respond? In many ways, it was Cronenberg's mature (and melancholic) response to the horror of his father's dying more than a decade earlier. As Cronenberg put it to Rodley, "Every love story must end tragically." The film's ending, with a final gesture of love and death, is profoundly moving.

Although Cronenberg insists that the film does not deal specifically with AIDS, it is hardly surprising that many audiences and critics understood it that way, given the social context. It was, in any case, widely praised by critics as Cronenberg's most tautly suspenseful, intellectually rigorous, and metaphorically stimulating film. He had transformed what might have been a routine Hollywood directing assignment into a rich, personal vision, framed by a touching love story.

DOUBLE TROUBLE: *DEAD RINGERS*

There have been numerous Hollywood films with twins as the central characters. A few have been comedies, but most have been thrillers emphasizing the differences between the twins, such as having one an innocent and the other a killer: good/bad mirror images. Cronenberg's interest in twins arose not from these filmic precursors but from a bizarre, real-life scandal and tragedy in 1975. This was the double suicide of twin gynaecologists and involved accusations of drug addiction and patient abuse. *Twins*, a rather unappealing novel, was published in 1977 and was loosely based on the case. In 1981, Hollywood producer Sylvio Tabet agreed to option the book and produce the film version. Because Cronenberg was then working on *Videodrome*, he asked his friend Norman Snider to write the script. Although the producer liked the script, Cronenberg did not, finding that it retained too much material from the book. Snider agreed to write a second draft without a fee. Cronenberg found this draft an improvement, but Tabet disagreed, insisting on proceeding with the first draft. The project floundered in 1982, with Tabet refusing to pay Cronenberg his fee.

A couple of years later, Marc Boyman (who had introduced *The Fly* script to Cronenberg) became involved and initiated a series of (invariably frustrating) meetings with Hollywood executives. Cronenberg told Brian Johnson that "They were worried that it would be too controversial." While some accepted the drug element, there was constant resistance to the bleakness of the story and to the gynaecology. Some even asked why the twins could not be lawyers, to which Cronenberg could only respond, "If you think they have to be lawyers, then you don't understand this project. . . ." One interested producer insisted on replacing Snider with a writer who would develop a less bleak script. The new script made the twins more normal and again failed to satisfy Cronenberg. He would likely have refused to direct it, but the company soon folded.

Oddly enough, given the debacle over *Total Recall*, the producer who finally picked up the project as Cronenberg conceived of it was Dino De Laurentiis. Cronenberg told Anne Billson that this was "because Dino is delightfully mad." Encouraged by the producer's commitment, Cronenberg wrote another version of the script, basing it on the earlier drafts by Snider. It now moved away from any sense of recreating the original story, retaining only the central premise of twin gynaecologists who abuse prescription drugs and become equal partners in schizophrenic doom. The twins were renamed "Mantle" — implying both a sense of concealment and of "mental." The explicit homosexuality of the book was eliminated, and the story became one more about homoerotic fantasy than about actual gayness. At De Laurentiis's suggestion, Cronenberg added a new dimension: the twins sharing the same lover, a famous actress, while pretending that they are the same person.

Cronenberg noted that it was very important to him that the twins were not only "two men forming a perfect unit that excluded everybody else" but that they were gynaecologists. He told Owen Gleiberman:

Directing Jeremy Irons on the set of Dead Ringers.

"The twins share not only one woman in particular sexually, but they share their understanding of women and their study of women. . . . It was obvious to me that my friends at school who were drawn to gynecology very often had serious trouble with women."

The Mantle twins are motivated by a mixture of fascination for, and fear of, women's bodies that drives their attempts at control. As critics were to note, this drive has clear overtones of contemporary feminist concerns about the power relations between male gynaecologists and their patients.

For Cronenberg, the issue of biological determinism (of twins and of males/females) was central. He believed that scientific research on twins proved his point. "It's very mysterious," he told Karen Jaehne, "but the implication of all this is that a huge amount of what we are is biologically predestined." He insisted that whether he favoured this view or not was irrelevant. "Like everybody else, I'm attached to the notion that I am free and that my will determines my own life, but maybe I'm wrong. There's a lot to be tested here." *Dead Ringers*, he remarked to Anne Billson, "is as close to a classical tragedy as I've come, in that it's inevitable right from the opening what the twins' destiny will be."

Preproduction for the film began in 1987 in Toronto with the construction of $300,000 worth of sets stored in a leased building. Suddenly the producers announced that they had to withdraw from the film. They had overextended themselves on several projects and were on the verge of bankruptcy. By an odd quirk of fate, Cronenberg received the news just as he was about to receive another honour in his native city. The Power Plant gallery of contemporary art in Toronto mounted an exhibition of his work, Crimes against Nature, bracketed with the comparable work of sculptor Mark Prent. (The exhibition included video extracts from Cronenberg's films using touch-screen computers for viewers' selections; the exploding-head scene from *Scanners* was by far the most popular choice.)

Faced with the equally unenviable alternatives of cancelling the "Twins" project and facing the cost of removing the sets or continuing to search for other financing, Cronenberg opted for the braver. He and Marc Boyman decided to produce the film themselves. It was, said Cronenberg to Rodley, "the beginning of ten months of agony like I've never experienced." Empty space in the leased building was rented to other producers, and his regular production team agreed to wait for new financing. The only exception was cinematographer Mark Irwin, who left Cronenberg after six films to take a job in the United States — a betrayal that considerably disturbed Cronenberg. Undoubtedly he survived the hiatus partly because of what Boyman described to Owen Gleiberman as his "terrific sense of humor and a fabulous brain."

Eventually the almost $13 million budget was put together from a mixture of Canadian, American, and British sources, mostly from presales of the distribution rights. Although it was a harrowing experience raising the money, Cronenberg noted to Billson that, as his own producer, "The good part is that, once you start to shoot, you have total control." With his usual quirky sense of humour, Cronenberg named their production company after the twins' clinic in the film: The Mantle Clinic II. During postproduction, Cronenberg agreed to drop the title "Twins" to accommodate his old friend, Ivan Reitman, who was working on a Hollywood film with the same title.

Hiring an actor for the role of the twins was a major problem. Cronenberg told Billson that he could not get an American actor whom he wanted. "Some were not available, some hated the script, but beyond that a lot of actors didn't want to play gynae-cologists. . . . A lot of actors who would be delighted to play Mafia hit men would *not* play gynaecologists." Another difficulty was that the role was a double one: "And that meant an actor was going to have to play a lot of scenes with himself in which he is not there, and that would be a big problem for a Method actor." Eventually Cronenberg decided that the classical training and discipline of the English acting style would be most appropriate. Jeremy Irons, then best known in North America for his roles in *Brideshead Revisited* and *The French Lieutenant's Woman*, was his first choice.

Irons later admitted that he had reservations about taking the role when he first read the script. "I was worried by the possibility of bad taste throughout it," he told Brian Johnson. "I happen to have a female agent, and a female wife, and they found the whole situation of gynecologists taking advantage of their patients very distasteful and very alarming — it's many women's nightmare." However, after meeting Cronenberg, he decided that he both liked him and trusted in his integrity. The relationship became so warm that Irons would later publicly thank Cronenberg at the Oscar ceremonies in 1990.

To prepare Irons for his role, Cronenberg had him read several books about twins as well as a textbook on gynaecology. On set, Irons was the disciplined, consummate professional that Cronenberg had expected. To show both twins on-screen at the same time, a sophisticated variation of the split-screen method was developed using a moving camera with a computer memory. This method made it possible for the camera to follow an identical path in different shots. Dialogue scenes between the twins had to be meticulously planned and staged. Irons had to deliver his lines to a double, then switch places, being careful to assume the double's exact position. "It was a great acting challenge," Irons later told Johnson. "It is very interesting to try and create a chemistry onscreen between oneself and oneself. The two characters became very separate to me, with very different energies."

Cronenberg's first choice for the twins' lover was Genevieve Bujold, but she, too, had reservations about accepting the role. Cronenberg well understood her hesitation. "Imagine her reading the script," he said to Johnson. "In her first scene, she's on a gynecological table with her legs up and she's being examined. She has to wonder, 'How am I going to handle that? Where's the camera going to be?' " As with Irons, Cronenberg met with her, explained how each scene would be filmed, and gained her trust.

FIGURE 20

*With Jeremy Irons and their Genie
Awards for* Dead Ringers *in 1989.*

Despite the earlier difficulties in mounting the production, the eleven-week shoot itself went remarkably smoothly. On a visit to the set, Karen Jaehne described the crew as "unusually disciplined and impressively organized." She noted the atmosphere:

> Cronenberg cracked jokes; producer Marc Boyman beamed like the sun into the cavernous studio they'd been supporting through long months of delayed start dates; the lean wit of Jeremy Irons mingled comfortably with the spare self-irony of the Canadian crew; Genevieve Bujold maintained her vows of silence like a nun, even if Irons' Mantle Clinic couture offered the comfort of a high priest in a surplice.

The reference was an apt one, for among the film's inventions are the scarlet robes that the twins' surgical team wears, like ecclesiastical robes, in the operating room. Cronenberg wanted the doctors to be like priests and cardinals, dedicated to the mysteries of their rituals.

Dead Ringers was selected to open the 1988 Toronto Festival of Festivals, and it received an enthusiastic reception. It went on to garner almost uniformly admiring reviews around the world and considerable commercial success. Critics were losing their obsession with detailing Cronenberg's obsessions and began drawing attention to his visual style. Although he has always had a strongly poetic sense of imagery, most critics only began noticing it after *Videodrome*. With *The Fly* and *Dead Ringers* it was obvious. *Dead Ringers* in particular was something of a return to the elegant precision of *Crimes of the Future*: the cool aquamarine of the Mantles' apartment, the scarlet priest-like robes of the operating room, the candlelighting in Claire's apartment. These and other elements emphasize the film's ambiguity and undermine attempts to locate a simple, naturalistic explanation of the events.

The Mantle twins were also seen as key characters in terms of understanding Cronenberg's explorations of masculinity. Like Max Renn and Seth Brundle, they are flawed, unstable, obsessed, and largely passive characters, alienated from women, if not terrified of them. The Mantles' attempt to form an exclusive "boys' club" leads, inexorably, to a horrifying self-destruction. As Pam Cook noted, the Cronenberg hero "acts out his death drive, striving to return to the intra-uterine haven he has longed for since birth." Cronenberg himself reflected something similar when he said to Rodley: "It has to do with this ineffable sadness that is an element of human existence."

A TRIBUTE TO BURROUGHS: *NAKED LUNCH*

It is hardly surprising that Cronenberg had long nursed an ambition to direct a film version of Burroughs's most famous novel. Burroughs had been one of his strongest conditioning influences, and many of his early films had included recognizable elements of Burroughsian imagery and ideas. They shared similar nightmares and visions. However, it was not until Cronenberg began to grow beyond Burroughs that he could contemplate writing and directing a film adaptation of *Naked Lunch*.

Cronenberg has always insisted that his relationship to Burroughs was one less of influence than of shared connections in terms of literary imagination. Yet the reflections of a Burroughsian universe in Cronenberg's early films are so pervasive that it is difficult to consider them as merely drawn from parallel lines of thought. At the same time, the personalities of the two men could not be more different. Burroughs was the quintessential rebel of the Beat generation, rejecting his upper middle-class background to become a wanderer and exile. He was a homosexual and a drug addict who went through several attempts to cure his addiction; he had accidentally shot and killed his wife before moving to live and write in Tangier. In no small measure, his writings (with their themes of sexuality, addiction, and control) are imaginative explorations of his own experiences. Cronenberg was born, and has remained, a solidly middle-class

Torontonian, a happy family man, whose rebellion against established values has been entirely sublimated in his art. He explained to John Harkness: "Burroughs confirmed my sense that the Eisenhower version of reality was not the only reality. There's this other stuff going on. . . . It was not a model for a lifestyle, it was the wildness of the imagination, the disease imagery."

The first steps toward the production of the film version of *Naked Lunch* were initiated by British producer Jeremy Thomas, who had met Cronenberg in 1984 at the Toronto Festival of Festivals. Although he, Cronenberg, and Burroughs visited Tangier the following year, the project was put on hold while Cronenberg worked on *The Fly* and *Dead Ringers*. Finally, in 1989, after Thomas had raised the initial financing, Cronenberg began working on the film adaptation.

He lived for a time in London, writing the first draft while playing the leading role in *Nightbreed*, directed by Clive Barker, a British horror writer and filmmaker. He was aware that the novel was unfilmable in any form of literal translation: it would be excessively long and would cost more than anyone had ever spent on a film. Cronenberg also did not want to focus on the social problem of drugs, preferring to emphasize Burroughs's drug imagery for his alter ego, Bill Lee, as metaphors of addiction, manipulation, and control. Eventually Cronenberg invented his own drugs so that "they would have internal, metaphorical connections" rather than social ones, as he described it to Rodley. He also knew that he wanted narrative cohesiveness and characters, especially a woman in a central role. (In the end, the film had two women, both played by Australian Judy Davis. Their introduction highlighted the fragility of Bill Lee's ego, much as a similar character had done for the Mantle twins.) Most of all, Cronenberg wanted it to focus on creativity and the act of writing: to become, in fact, a film *about* Burroughs. He explained to John Harkness:

"I wanted to do something that connected with Burroughs as an influence on me, to get at how much of the book has

FIGURE 21

With William Burroughs during production of Naked Lunch.

been absorbed by the culture, at the iconic element of Burroughs as a figure, things you would not get if you transcribed the book. I was trying to get to the sensibility of the man."

The script that emerged blended imagery and portions of the novel with some of Burroughs's other works, including the earlier *Junkie* and the later *Exterminator!*. Cronenberg also considerably muted the novel's aggressive homosexuality (as he had done earlier with "Twins") — much to the later chagrin of several gay critics. He explained to Chris Rodley that this muting came from his attempt "to fuse my own sensibility with Burroughs and create a third thing that neither he nor I would have done on his own." It also came from his understanding of the difference between Burroughs the writer and the particular work itself. He had discussed with Burroughs that he himself was not gay and that his own sexuality would affect the film's sexuality. Burroughs contributed nothing directly to the script beyond giving his approval.

Cronenberg had intended to write a script that avoided special effects. He later told Rick Groen that he was surprised to discover, as he wrote, that "creatures started to appear and talk" — not only the Mugwumps and giant centipedes from Burroughs but also typewriters that mutate into talking bugs. In particular, he wanted the sex to have "metaphoric value," but he felt that having the actors "groping each other" was "too real and you lose the metaphor. So I showed it through the creatures."

Raising the more than $20 million financing for the project proved difficult and took time. In fact, the production temporarily went into limbo when some Japanese investors withdrew, and new financing had to be found. During this interval, Cronenberg made several television commercials and two hour-long dramas for the CBC's Scales of Justice series. Although he did not contribute to the scripts, on both *Regina versus Horvath* and *Regina versus Logan* he was able to work with several familiar members of his team, including Carol Spier, Howard Shore, and Ron Sanders.

One reason that he took on the two CBC productions was to keep his team together while *Naked Lunch* was refinanced. All his team members are well aware that he is generous in returning the loyalty they give him. Cronenberg also discovered that the time pressures of filming for television necessitated changes in his usual approaches to directing.

Naked Lunch finally went into production in January 1991 as a Canadian-British coproduction. Cronenberg had intended to shoot interiors in Toronto and exteriors in Tangier, where Burroughs had written the novel. The Gulf crisis prevented that approach, and Cronenberg was forced into an instant rewrite of the script. Although initially depressed, he quickly realized that he had been seduced by the biographical element (visiting Tangier in 1985 with Burroughs). "He would take his cane and point where he and Kerouac drank, where he wrote Naked Lunch and where he met Paul Bowles," Cronenberg told Harkness. He realized that Interzone "needed to be a state of mind," not a real place to which Bill Lee flees. "There always was the suggestion that he never left New York at all. . . ." Being forced to abandon location shooting was pure serendipity: the use of constructed sets emphasizes the film's hallucinatory claustrophobia, its sense of Lee being trapped, passively, in his own paranoid fantasies. The sets also accentuate Cronenberg's structure: a narrative told relentlessly from Lee's point of view — much as he had done with Max Renn in the latter part of *Videodrome*. The narrative structure also enabled Cronenberg to use the film's creatures to embody the characters' sexuality. He explained this device to Breskin as giving the audience

> the same sort of avoidance-denial level cinematically that I'm saying Lee is doing psycho-emotionally. . . . I'm saying Lee is denying and avoiding certain realities about himself. And to the extent that he is controlling his fantasies, they are also avoiding, denying fantasies.

This statement clearly expresses the mature insight that Cronenberg was bringing to his work, as well as to that of Burroughs.

Selected to play the role of Lee, the Burroughs surrogate, was Peter Weller, fresh from the set of *Robocop 2*. Weller told Rob Salem that he first read the novel in 1968 when he was twenty. "It was like the Bible to me; the ultimate novel of disobedience." Weller heard about the project by chance from cinematographer Mark Irwin during production of *Robocop 2*. "I immediately wrote to Cronenberg," he told Salem, "and I said 'I dig it. I love your stuff and this book is a Bible to me. So if you haven't cast it, I want to be the guy.'" Weller also recognized that Cronenberg's approach to adapting the novel was the only way that it could be filmed, and he preferred the use of fake drugs because "It's the addiction that's important." Both comments reflect the benefits of Cronenberg's collaborative work with actors in terms of discussing his approach to a film so that there is a shared understanding.

Naked Lunch was released in January 1992. Reviews were largely positive, praising the film's daring inventiveness, though many critics insisted that the film was mystifying to those lacking knowledge of Burroughs and his life. Audiences tended to agree. *Naked Lunch* might be Cronenberg's most cerebral and passionate work, but it did not appeal to audiences and, despite the praise of critics, did not do well at the box office.

Cronenberg, however, was moving on to his next project. In late 1992, he began filming an adaptation of the successful stage play *M. Butterfly*, by David Henry Hwang. Financed by Warner Brothers, scripted by Cronenberg and Hwang, it features John Lone and Jeremy Irons. Both Irons and Cronenberg expressed their pleasure in being able to work together again. The film was shot in Budapest (standing in for Paris), China, and studios in Toronto. Its story seems well suited to Cronenberg's sensibility: it tells of René Gallimard (played by Irons), a French diplomat in Beijing, who falls in love with a male Beijing Opera performer, convinced that he is a woman. No doubt Gallimard is another Cronenberg hero trapped within his own delusions. Cronenberg has said that, while the subversive elements of the play have been retained, his adaptation is less schematic and more emotional than the original. Completed in late summer 1993, it was selected as the opening film for Toronto's Festival of Festivals — the second time that one of Cronenberg's films has been thus honoured. It was released commercially in September 1993.

In the summer of 1993, Cronenberg announced a new project: a revival of his idea for a television series similar to that spurned by American television a decade earlier. *Crimes against Nature* will feature "a strange cop" fighting crime in the "slightly dislocated universe" of Toronto. Produced by Toronto-based Paragon Entertainment, and with a broadcast agreement with CBC Television, the series is scheduled to begin shooting in February 1994. Cronenberg will both write and direct the projected six episodes of the series. He believes that Canadian television is becoming more liberal and creative in the battle to attract viewers. The CBC in particular, he said, has always opened its doors to alternative programming. Viewers will await with interest Cronenberg's foray into the well-known minefield of network television drama. Several well-known directors before him have attempted to overcome the difficulties. None could be said to have entirely succeeded.

THE ARTIST AS DERELICT

Bill Lee in *Naked Lunch* is only the latest in a long line of derelicts, misfits, and outsiders who have crossed the screen in the films of David Cronenberg. They first appeared as peripheral metaphors: the unknown experimental subjects in *Stereo*, the garbage-truck ending of *Rabid*, the brood lair of *The Brood* — and not least the TV-addicted derelicts of *Videodrome*. They became pivotal in *Scanners*, in which Cameron Vale and the other scanners are described as "social misfits." However, since Max Renn in *Videodrome* (described by one character as "like my father's derelicts"), Cronenberg's films have been dominated by male protagonists characterized by a sense of dereliction. Although Renn, Brundle, the Mantle twins, and Lee are very different characters, they are isolated from the social world, abandoned to their personal demons. It is no surprise to learn that Cronenberg told Rick Groen that he considers his two literary heroes, Nabokov and Burroughs, "both aliens in America — Burroughs from the inside and Nabokov from the outside." For Cronenberg, from the perspective of what he acknowledged to David Breskin as his *"astringent romanticism,"* his characters are images of the artist as social misfit, doomed to create and equally doomed to fail. He said to Tim Lucas that "all the fabled American artists became derelicts." In the interview with Groen, he explained that "most of the greatest writers in American literature — Hawthorne, Melville, Whitman — all died feeling wretched, feeling that they hadn't achieved anything. It seems almost an inevitable thing in an artist." If the point is exaggerated, it is also an intimation of his romantic sensibility and his own "black *sun.*" Cronenberg also told Groen that he thinks "at some distant point that I could look back, and dismiss all my work as egregious" — though not while ". . . I'm still excited about making other films." Despite his success, he has continued to feel that he is an outsider.

Although Cronenberg has often spoken of art as necessarily socially disruptive and dangerous, he also thinks that it has a totemic function, able to keep danger at a distance. He thinks of his films as akin to the play of children or animals, rehearsing for the realities of later life. He said to Groen: "In a way my movies are an incantation against things that I don't want to happen but whose existence I have to acknowledge. Things like death or disease or the loss of your children." Curiously, perhaps, these incantations are without hope; his isolated, passive, obsessed characters are destroyed by the attributes that he has used to define them. Like the romantic artists he refers to, they are doomed as derelicts.

Despite Cronenberg's clear identification with his characters, he is nothing like them in real life. He said to Breskin, for example, that he has "a real *horror* of passivity. . . . I don't like fantasy in my life. I have an incredible abhorrence of that, and a real drive into reality." Similarly, he lives happily in Toronto, a city whose "clean-shaven, pink-faced, respectably dressed" virtue has often served Cronenberg as a metaphor of the neatness and order that mask the demons and repressions of his characters. He would still acknowledge the comment that he made fifteen years ago to Katherine Govier that the rich houses in Toronto's Forest Hill are full of "crazy people, all going through the most blood-curdling things." The chaos in his films is a perverted reflection of his sense of order. He separates his life and his art by suggesting that, as a citizen and a father, he has social responsibilities, but the artist's only "responsibility is to be irresponsible," as he put it to Breskin.

We might think of his passion for racing cars as a metaphor for his sense of order and chaos, control and freedom. He likes to drive fast cars, he told Karen Jaehne,

"because it's a form of freedom, and you're testing your own control over a situation that has not been deemed safe. When you drive within the speed limit, it's not your own will that is keeping your life intact; it has been imposed. When you transgress that, you are reclaiming total control of a very specific situation."

As Jaehne remarked, it is as though Cronenberg embodies a peculiar Canadian paradox: the instinct to conform while simultaneously resisting conformity in a radical way. His friend Norman Snider told Colapinto that the key to understanding Cronenberg "is that co-existing with all the weirdness is a guy who believes in certain sturdy values. He really believes in equilibrium and balance. In a sense, David is the all-Canadian boy."

A delicate balance: detachment and passionate engagement; reason and emotion; mind and body; art as both disease and cure; science and art; a male unmasking the weaknesses of masculinity; ambitious and outspoken about his work but intensely private about his personal life; the creator of films whose passive, powerless heroes are the antithesis of his own enterprising creativity; life that can only end in failure yet must be lived with passion; a devoted middle-class husband and father whose films are the scourge of middle-class values; paradoxes that are more apparent than real.

It is as though, as an adolescent, Cronenberg had taken to heart the century-old advice of Gustave Flaubert: "Be regular and orderly in your life, like a bourgeois, so that you may be violent and original in your work."

And, no doubt, David Cronenberg will continue to astonish us.

CHRONOLOGY

1943   David Cronenberg is born in Toronto, Ontario, on 15 March.

1962   *Naked Lunch* is published in the United States and stirs a major literary controversy.

1963   Cronenberg is admitted to the University of Toronto as an honours science student.

1964   He wins the Epstein Award for a short story and transfers to honours English language and literature. The Isaacs Gallery in Toronto organizes two screenings of Canadian experimental films.

1965   Cronenberg is awarded the Gertrude Lawler Scholarship for finishing first at University College. He travels in Europe for several months, returning to university studies the following year. David Secter, a University of Toronto student, completes a feature film, *Winter Kept Us Warm*. The Bohemian Embassy coffeehouse in Toronto begins regular screenings of American underground films.

1966   Cronenberg makes his first short film, *Transfer*. He and other student and independent filmmakers establish the Film-Makers Co-operative (later renamed the Canadian Filmmakers' Distribution Centre). A Canadian film magazine, *Take One*, is first published.

1967   Cronenberg graduates from the University of Toronto with a general B.A. He also completes his second short film, *From the Drain*. The federal government creates the Canadian Film Development Corporation (CFDC) (later renamed Telefilm Canada) to assist the financing of feature-film production. In Toronto, Cinecity theatre organizes Cinethon, a marathon weekend festival of American and Canadian underground films, including *Transfer*.

1968   Cronenberg enrols in the M.A. English graduate program (make-up year).

1969   He makes his first long film, *Stereo*, in 35mm black and white, partially funded by a Canada Council writing grant. Canadian and foreign critical reaction at festivals is highly positive. It is one of ten Canadian films selected to represent "New Cinema" around the world at screenings in Brussels, Belgium.

1970   Cronenberg marries Margaret Hindson. He makes his first 35mm colour feature film, *Crimes of the Future*, partially funded by investment from the CFDC. He also receives a Canada Council grant, lives for nearly a year in the south of France, writes a draft of a novel, and directs three short "fillers" for CBC Television.

1971   He returns to Toronto and directs six more "fillers" for CBC Television and a short television drama, *Secret Weapons*.

1972   He begins work on a script for a feature film, *Shivers* (originally titled "Orgy of the Blood Parasites"). A daughter, Cassandra, is born.

1973   His father dies. Cronenberg completes the script of *Shivers* and offers it to producers John Dunning and André Link of the Montreal company Cinépix. Although they are interested, financing is difficult to obtain.

1974   Cronenberg travels to Los Angeles to offer the script there. The CFDC finally agrees to invest in *Shivers*. The film is shot in Montreal in August and September on a budget of approximately $180,000.

1975   *Shivers* is released (originally titled *The Parasite Murders*). Robert Fulford (as Marshall Delaney) writes a notorious review, describing it as the most repulsive film he had ever seen. Other critics disagree, considering the film an extension of Cronenberg's earlier work. The film was eventually released in forty countries (including the States, where it was retitled *They Came from Within*), bringing a financial return of some $5 million and making it the most commercially successful film in which the CFDC had invested. Cronenberg directs two short dramas for CBC Television: *The Victim* and *The Lie Chair*. He begins work for Cinépix on a second feature, *Rabid*. *Shivers* is rejected from competing in the Canadian Film Awards.

1976   He directs a short drama for CBC Television, *The Italian Machine*, and directs *Rabid* in Montreal in November on a budget of $530,000, with indirect CFDC participation. Changes in Canada's tax laws introduce the capital cost allowance to encourage private investment in feature-film production.

1977   *Rabid* is released and eventually grosses about $7 million worldwide. Cronenberg buys a house in Toronto and writes the script for *The Brood* following an acrimonious divorce and child-custody dispute.

1978   He shoots *Fast Company* in July and August in Calgary and Edmonton, Alberta at a cost of $1.2 million. He shoots *The Brood* in Toronto in November and December at a cost of $1.4 million.

1979   *Fast Company* and *The Brood* are released. Cronenberg writes *Scanners* based on the earlier scripts "Telepathy 2000" and "The Sensitives." The film is shot from October to December in Montreal at a cost of $4.1 million. Cronenberg marries Carolyn Zeifman. The Academy of Canadian Cinema is incorporated.

1980   Cronenberg announces plans to film a version of Mary Shelley's *Frankenstein*, but the project does not materialize. He begins writing the script for what later becomes *Videodrome*. The Academy of Canadian Cinema introduces the Genie Awards to replace the former Etrogs and Canadian Film Awards.

1981	*Scanners* is released and is a major commercial success. *Videodrome* is shot in Toronto from October to December at a cost of $6 million. Cronenberg begins work with various scriptwriters on the "Twins" project that is eventually filmed as *Dead Ringers*.
1983	*Videodrome* is released. It is praised by most critics but does not do well at the box office. Cronenberg directs *The Dead Zone* in Toronto and southern Ontario from January to March on a budget of $10 million. In September, the Festival of Festivals mounts a retrospective in Toronto of Cronenberg's films, and the Academy of Canadian Cinema publishes *The Shape of Rage: The Films of David Cronenberg*. *The Dead Zone* is released.
1984	Cronenberg wins a Genie Award as Best Director for *Videodrome*. He begins working with Hollywood producer Dino De Laurentiis on several projects, including *Total Recall*, but they cannot agree on the script. (The film is eventually directed by Paul Verhoeven in 1990.) He holds discussions with British producer Jeremy Thomas concerning the possibility of filming William S. Burroughs's novel *Naked Lunch*, a project that Cronenberg had first proposed in 1981.
1985	Cronenberg makes a cameo acting appearance in *Into the Night*, directed by John Landis. Numerous possible directing projects do not materialize until he is offered the script for *The Fly*. He accepts it but insists on rewriting it. *The Fly* is shot in Toronto and at the Kleinburg studios north of Toronto on a budget of $10 million.
1986	*The Fly* is released and is a major critical and financial success, grossing about $100 million at the box office. Cronenberg begins work again on "Twins" (later retitled *Dead Ringers*).
1987	With sets already constructed, the film's main investor, Dino De Laurentiis, is forced to withdraw because of financial problems. Cronenberg and Marc Boyman

raise financing (approximately $13 million) in order to produce the film themselves. In October, The Power Plant art gallery in Toronto includes Cronenberg's work in a joint exhibition with works by sculptor Mark Prent and publishes a catalogue, *Prent/Cronenberg: Crimes against Nature*.

1988   In September, *Dead Ringers* is selected to open the Toronto Festival of Festivals: it gains considerable critical acclaim and later becomes a major international critical and commercial success.

1989   Cronenberg wins his second Genie Award as Best Director for *Dead Ringers*. He directs three commercials for Ontario Hydro. In London, England, he writes the first draft of the screenplay for *Naked Lunch* while playing the lead role in *Nightbreed*, directed by Clive Barker.

1990   While financing for *Naked Lunch* is raised and the production is planned, Cronenberg directs three commercials (for Caramilk and Nike) and two hour-long docudramas for the CBC series Scales of Justice. In November, a major retrospective of Cronenberg's films opens in Paris, France. He receives France's prestigious Chevalier de l'ordre des arts et des lettres.

1991   Production of *Naked Lunch* begins in Toronto on a budget of $17 million American as a British-Canadian coproduction. The script is rewritten because of the impossibility of filming on location in Tangier due to the Gulf crisis.

1992   *Naked Lunch* is released. Cronenberg wins an unprecedented third Genie Award as Best Director for *Naked Lunch*. He begins work on his next project, an adaptation of *M. Butterfly*, the successful Broadway play by David Henry Hwang. The film features Jeremy Irons and John Lone. Cronenberg plays the leading role in *Blue*, a short film by Don McKellar.

1993   Cronenberg films *M. Butterfly* in Asia, Budapest, and at

CineSpace Studios in Toronto; postproduction is completed in Toronto. In Tokyo, Japan, a retrospective of all Cronenberg's films opens in March, together with an exhibition of props and set designs. The exhibition is also presented at the Royal Ontario Museum in September. *M. Butterfly* is selected to open Toronto's Festival of Festivals in September and is released commercially immediately after this première. Cronenberg announces that his next project is a television series, *Crimes against Nature*, to begin filming in Toronto in February 1994.

THE FILMS OF DAVID CRONENBERG

1966

Transfer

Director, Screenplay, Cinematography, Editor: David Cronenberg
Sound: Margaret Hindson, Stephen Nosko
Cast: Mort Ritts, Rafe Macpherson
7 mins.

1967

From the Drain

Director, Screenplay, Cinematography, Editor: David Cronenberg
Cast: Mort Ritts, Stephen Nosko
14 mins.

1969

Stereo

Production company: Emergent Films
*Producer, Director, Screenplay, Cinematography (black and white),
   Editor*: David Cronenberg
Production assistants: Stephen Nosko, Pedro McCormick, Janet
   G.M. Good
Cast: Ronald Mlodzik, Iain Ewing, Jack Messinger, Clara Mayer,
   Paul Mulholland, Arlene Mlodzik, Glenn McCauley, and others
65 mins.

1970

Crimes of the Future

Production company: Emergent Films, with the participation of
the Canadian Film Development Corporation (CFDC)
Producer, Director, Screenplay, Cinematography, Editor: David Cronenberg
Production assistant: Stephen Nosko
Titles: Jon Lidolt
Cast: Ronald Mlodzik (*Adrian Tripod*), John Lidolt, Tania Zolty,
Jack Messinger, Iain Ewing, Rafe Macpherson, Willem Poolman, Donald Owen, Norman Snider, Stephen Czernecki, and
others
65 mins.

1971

THREE 16MM fillers for canadian television

Jim Ritchie Sculptor

Letter from Michelangelo

(text: Michelangelo)

Tourettes

Director, Screenplay, Cinematography: David Cronenberg

1972

SIX 16MM fillers for canadian television

Don Valley

Fort York

Lakeshore

Winter Garden

Scarborough Bluffs

In the Dirt

Director, Screenplay, Cinematography: David Cronenberg

Secret Weapons

Production company: Emergent Films for the Canadian Broadcasting Corporation (CBC) (Program X)
Executive producer: Paddy Simpson
Associate producer: George Jonas
Director, Cinematography: David Cronenberg
Screenplay: Norman Snider
Commentary: Lister Sinclair
Cast: Barbara O'Kelly (*motorcycle-gang leader*), Norman Snider (*the scientist*), Vernon Chapman (*the bureaucrat*), Ronald Mlodzik, Bruce Martin, Tom Skudra, Moses Smith, Michael D. Spencer, G. Chalmers Adams
27 mins.

1975

Shivers (also known as *They Came from Within, The Parasite Murders*)

Production company: DAL Productions Ltd., with the participation of the CFDC
Producers: Ivan Reitman, John Dunning, André Link
Director, Screenplay: David Cronenberg
Cinematography: Robert Saad
Sound: Michael Higgs
Editor: Patrick Dodd
Music: Ivan Reitman

Special makeup and creatures: Joe Blasco
Cast: Paul Hampton (*Roger St. Luc*), Joe Silver (*Rollo Linsky*), Lynn Lowry (*Forsythe*), Allan Migicovsky (*Nicholas Tudor*), Susan Petrie (*Janine Tudor*), Barbara Steele (*Betts*), Ronald Mlodzik (*Merrick*), Barrie Baldero (*Detective Heller*), Camille Ducharme (*Mr. Guilbault*), Hanka Posnanka (*Mrs. Guilbault*), and others
87 mins.

The Victim

Production company: CBC (Peep Show)
Executive producer: George Bloomfield
Producer: Deborah Peaker
Director: David Cronenberg
Screenplay: Ty Haller
Cameras: Eamonn Beglan, Ron Manson, John Halenda, Dave Doherty, Peter Brimson
Sound: Brian Radford, Bill Dunn
Videotape editor: Garry Fisher
Art director: Nickolai Soliov
Cast: Janet Wright (*Lucy*), Johnathan Welsh (*Donald*), Cedric Smith (*man on park bench*)
27 mins.

The Lie Chair

Production company: CBC (Peep Show)
Executive producer: George Bloomfield
Producer: Eoin Sprott
Director: David Cronenberg
Screenplay: David Cole
Cameras: Eamonn Beglan, George Clemens, Tom Farquharson, Peter Brimson
Sound: Roland Huebsche, Bill Dunn
Set designer: Rudi Dorn
Cast: Richard Monette (*Neil*), Susan Hogan (*Carol*), Amelia Hall (*Mildred*), Doris Petrie (*Mrs. Rogers*)
27 mins.

1976

The Italian Machine

Production company: CBC (Teleplay)
Executive producer: Stephen Patrick
Director, Screenplay: David Cronenberg
Photography: Nicholas Evdemon
Sound: Tom Bilenky
Editor: David Denovan
Music consultant: Patrick Russell
Art director: Peter Douet
Cast: Gary McKeehan (*Lionel*), Frank Moore (*Fred*), Hardee Linehan
(*Bug*), Chuck Shamata (*Reinhardt*), Louis Negin (*Mouette*), Taby
Tarnow (*Lana*), Geza Kovacs (*Ricardo*), Cedrick Smith (*Luke*)
28 mins.

Rabid

Production company: Cinema Entertainment Enterprises (for DAL
Productions Ltd.), with the participation of the CFDC
Executive producers: André Link, Ivan Reitman
Producer: John Dunning
Director, Screenplay: David Cronenberg
Cinematography: René Verzier
Sound: Richard Lightstone
Editor: Jean Lafleur
Music: Ivan Reitman
Art director: Claude Marchand
Special makeup design: Joe Blasco Makeup Associates
Cast: Marilyn Chambers (*Rose*), Frank Moore (*Hart Read*), Joe
Silver (*Murray Cypher*), Howard Ryshpan (*Dr. Dan Keloid*), Patricia
Gage (*Dr. Roxanne Keloid*), Susan Roman (*Mindy Kent*), J. Roger
Periard (*Lloyd Walsh*), Lynne Deragon (*nurse Louise*), Terry
Schonblum (*Judy Glasberg*), Victor Desy (*Claude Lepointe*), and
others
91 mins.

1979

Fast Company

Production company: Michael Lebowitz Inc. (for Quadrant Films
Ltd.), with the participation of the CFDC
Executive producer: David M. Perlmutter
Producers: Michael Lebowitz, Peter O'Brian, Courtney Smith
Director: David Cronenberg
Screenplay: Phil Savath, Courtney Smith, David Cronenberg,
from an original story by Alan Treen
Cinematography: Mark Irwin
Sound: Bryan Day
Editor: Ronald Sanders
Music: Fred Mollin
Art director: Carol Spier
Cast: William Smith (*Lonnie Johnson*), Claudia Jennings (*Sammy*),
John Saxon (*Phil Adamson*), Nicholas Campbell (*Billy Brooker*),
Cedrick Smith (*Gary Black*), Judy Foster (*Candy*), George Buza
(*Meatball*), Robert Haley (*P.J.*), David Graham (*Stoner*), Don
Francks (*"Elder"*), and others
91 mins.

The Brood

Production companies: Les Productions Mutuelles and Elgin Inter-
national Productions, with the participation of the CFDC
Executive producers: Victor Solnicki, Pierre David
Producer: Claude Heroux
Director, Screenplay: David Cronenberg
Cinematography: Mark Irwin
Sound: Bryan Day
Editor: Alan Collins
Music: Howard Shore
Art Director: Carol Spier
Special makeup: Jack Young, Dennis Pike
Cast: Oliver Reed (*Dr. Hal Raglan*), Samantha Eggar (*Nola Carveth*),

Art Hindle (*Frank Carveth*), Cindy Hinds (*Candice Carveth*), Henry Beckman (*Barton Kelly*), Nuala Fitzgerald (*Juliana Kelly*), Susan Hogan (*Ruth Mayer*), Michael Magee (*Inspector Mrazek*), Joseph Shaw (*Dr. Desborough, coroner*), Gary McKeehan (*Mike Trellan*), and others

91 mins.

1980

Scanners

Production company: Filmplan International Inc., with the participation of the CFDC

Executive producers: Pierre David, Victor Solnicki

Producer: Claude Heroux

Director, Screenplay: David Cronenberg

Cinematography: Mark Irwin

Sound: Don Cohen

Editor: Ron Sanders

Music: Howard Shore

Art director: Carol Spier

Special makeup: Stephan Dupuis, Chris Walas, Tom Schwartz

Cast: Jennifer O'Neill (*Kim Obrist*), Stephen Lack (*Cameron Vale*), Patrick McGoohan (*Dr. Paul Ruth*), Lawrence Z. Dane (*Braedon Keller*), Michael Ironside (*Darryl Revok*), Robert Silverman (*Benjamin Pierce*), Adam Ludwig (*Arno Crostic*), Mavor Moore (*Trevellyan*), Fred Doederlein (*Dieter Tautz*), Sony Forbes (*invader*), and others

103 mins.

1982

Videodrome

Production company: Filmplan International II Inc., with the participation of the CFDC

Executive producers: Pierre David, Victor Solnicki
Producer: Claude Heroux
Director, Screenplay: David Cronenberg
Cinematography: Mark Irwin
Sound: Bryan Day
Editor: Ron Sanders
Music: Howard Shore
Art director: Carol Spier
Special makeup: Rick Baker
Cast: James Woods (*Max Renn*), Sonja Smits (*Bianca O'Blivion*), Deborah Harry (*Nicki Brand*), Peter Dvorsky (*Harlan*), Les Carlson (*Barry Convex*), Jack Creley (*Brian O'Blivion*), Lynne Gorman (*Masha*), Julie Khaner (*Bridey*), Reiner Shwarz (*Moses*), David Bolt (*Raphael*), and others
87 mins.

1983

The Dead Zone

Production company: Dead Zone Productions, in association with Lorimar Productions Inc.
Executive producer: Dino De Laurentiis
Producer: Debra Hill
Director: David Cronenberg
Screenplay: Jeffrey Boam, from a book by Stephen King
Cinematography: Mark Irwin
Sound: Bryan Day
Editor: Ron Sanders
Music: Michael Kamen
Production design: Carol Spier
Cast: Christopher Walken (*Johnny Smith*), Brooke Adams (*Sarah Bracknell*), Martin Sheen (*Greg Stillson*), Sean Sullivan (*Herb Smith*), Jackie Burroughs (*Vera Smith*), Herbert Lom (*Dr. Sam Weizak*), Tom Skerritt (*Bannerman*), Anthony Zerbe (*Roger*

Stuart), Nicholas Campbell (*Frank Dodd*), Peter Dvorsky
(*Dardis*), and others
100 mins.

1986

The Fly

Production company: Brooksfilms
Producer: Stuart Cornfeld
Director: David Cronenberg
Screenplay: Charles Edward Pogue, David Cronenberg, from a
    story by George Langelaan
Cinematography: Mark Irwin
Sound: Bryan Day
Editor: Ronald Sanders
Music: Howard Shore
Production design: Carol Spier
The fly created and designed by Chris Walas Inc.
Cast: Jeff Goldblum (*Seth Brundle*), Geena Davis (*Veronica Quaife*),
    John Getz (*Stathis Borans*), Joy Boushel (*Tawny*), Les Carlson
    (*Dr. Cheevers*), George Chuvalo (*Marky*), Michael Copeman
    (*second man in bar*), David Cronenberg (*gynaecologist*), Carol
    Lazare (*nurse*), Shawn Hewitt (*clerk*), and others
92 mins.

1988

Dead Ringers

Production company: Mantle Clinic II Ltd., in association with
    Morgan Creek Productions Inc., with the participation of
    Telefilm Canada
Executive producers: Carol Baum, Sylvio Tabet
Producers: David Cronenberg, Marc Boyman

Director: David Cronenberg
Screenplay: David Cronenberg, Norman Snider, based on the book *Twins* by Bari Wood and Jack Geasland
Cinematography: Peter Suschitzky
Sound: Bryan Day
Editor: Ronald Sanders
Music: Howard Shore
Production design: Carol Spier
Cast: Jeremy Irons (*Elliot and Beverly Mantle*), Genevieve Bujold (*Claire Niveau*), Heidi von Palleske (*Cary*), Barbara Gordon (*Danuta*), Shirley Douglas (*Laura*), Stephen Lack (*Anders Wolleck*), Nick Nichols (*Leo*), Lynn Cormack (*Arlene*), Damir Andrei (*Birchall*), Miriam Newhouse (*Mrs. Bookman*), and others
115 mins.

1989

Hydro

(Four commercials for Ontario Hydro)

1990

Caramilk

(Two commercials for William Neilson)

Nike

(Five commercials)

Regina versus Horvath

Production company: CBC, in association with Scales of Justice Enterprises Inc.
Executive in charge of production: Carol Reynolds
Producer: George Jonas
Director: David Cronenberg

Screenplay: Michael Tait, George Jonas
Photography: Rodney Charters
Sound: Bryan Day
Supervising editor: Ronald Sanders
Music: Howard Shore
Production design: Carol Spier
Cast: Justin Louis (*John Horvath*), Les Carlson (*Larry Proke*), Len Doncheff (*John Molnar*), Kurt Reis (*Mr. Justice Gould*), Michael Caruana (*Mr. R.D. Shantz, crown*), David Gardner (*Mr. D.G.G. Milne, defence*), James Edmond (*Dr. Gordon Stephenson, psychiatrist*), Frank Perry (*Dr. Coady, coroner*), and others
48 mins.

Regina versus Logan

Production company: CBC, in association with Scales of Justice Enterprises Inc.
Executive in charge of production: Carol Reynolds
Producer: George Jonas
Director: David Cronenberg
Screenplay: Gabriel Emmanuel, George Jonas
Photography: Rodney Charters
Sound: Bryan Day
Supervising editor: Ronald Sanders
Music: Howard Shore
Production design: Carol Spier
Cast: Barbara Turnbull (*as herself*), Richard Yearwood (*Cliff*), Desmond Campbell (*Hugh*), Mark Ferguson (*Warren*), and others
44 mins.

1991

Naked Lunch

Production company: Recorded Picture Company, with the participation of Telefilm Canada and the Ontario Film Development Corporation

Producer: Jeremy Thomas
Coproducer: Gabriella Martinelli
Director: David Cronenberg
Screenplay: David Cronenberg, based on the novel *Naked Lunch*
by William S. Burroughs
Cinematography: Peter Suschitzky
Sound: Bryan Day
Editor: Ronald Sanders
Music: Howard Shore
Production design: Carol Spier
Creatures created and designed by Chris Walas Inc.
Special-effects supervisor: Jim Isaac
Cast: Peter Weller (*Bill Lee*), Judy Davis (*Joan Lee, Joan Frost*), Roy
Scheider (*Dr. Benway*), Ian Holm (*Tom Frost*), Julian Sands (*Yves Cloquet*), Michael Zelnicker (*Martin*), Nicholas Campbell (*Hank*), Monique Mercure (*Fadela*), Joseph Scorsiani (*Kiki*), and others
115 mins.

1993

M. Butterfly

Production companies: Geffen Pictures, M. Butterfly Productions
Producer: Gabriella Martinelli
Director: David Cronenberg
Screenplay: David Henry Hwang, based on his original play
Cinematography: Peter Suschitzky
Editor: Ronald Sanders
Music: Howard Shore
Art Director: Carol Spier
Sound: Bryan Day
Cast: Jeremy Irons (*René Gallimard*), John Lone (*Song LiLing*), Barbara Sukowa (*Mme. Gallimard*), Annabel Leventon, Ian Richardson, and others
102 mins.

WORKS CONSULTED

Adilman, Sid. "David Cronenberg Japanese Style." *Toronto Star* 14 Mar. 1993: E1, E16.

Beard, Bill. "David Cronenberg's Fast Company." Rev. of *Fast Company*. *Cinema Canada* Sept. 1979: 32–33.

Beard, William. "The Visceral Mind: The Major Films of David Cronenberg." Handling 1–79.

Beattie, Eleanor. *A Handbook of Canadian Film*. Take One Film Book Series 2. Toronto: Martin; Montreal: Take One, 1973.

_____ . *The Handbook of Canadian Film*. 2nd ed. Take One Film Book Series 4. Toronto: Martin; Montreal: Take One, 1977.

Beker, Marilyn. "David Cronenberg." *Expression* Mar.–Apr. 1989: 148–56.

Billson, Anne. "Cronenberg on Cronenberg: A Career in Stereo." *Monthly Film Bulletin* Jan. 1989: 4–6.

Braun, E. "The Gentle Art of Mind Boggling." *Films* 1.7 (1981): 22–25.

Briggs, Peter. "Crimes of the Future." Rev. of *Crimes of the Future*. *Take One* 2.6 (1969): 21.

Brooke, Rupert. *Letters from America*. London: Sidgwick, 1916.

Burroughs, William S. *Naked Lunch*. 1959. New York: Grove, 1966.

Chesley, Stephen. "It'll Bug You." *Cinema Canada* Oct. 1975: 23–25.

Chute, David. "David Cronenberg's Gore-Tech Visions." *Rolling Stone* 17 Mar. 1983: 33, 36.

_____ . "He Came from Within." *Film Comment* Mar.–Apr. 1980: 36–39, 42.

_____ . "Twelve New Movies: The Latest from Cronenberg and Venice." *Film Comment* Jan.–Feb. 1982: 2, 4. [Venice segment, 4+, by Harlan Kennedy.]

Clandfield, David. *Canadian Film*. Perspectives on Canadian Culture series. Toronto: Oxford UP, 1987.

Cocteau, Jean. *The Journals of Jean Cocteau*. London: Museum, 1957.

Colapinto, John. "Horror Show." *Saturday Night* Oct. 1986: 40+.

Combs, Richard. "Rabid." Rev. of *Rabid*. *Monthly Film Bulletin* Nov. 1977: 240.

_____. "Shivers." Rev. of *Shivers*. *Monthly Film Bulletin* Mar. 1976: 62.

Cook, Pam. "Dead Ringers." Rev. of *Dead Ringers*. *Monthly Film Bulletin* Jan. 1989: 3–4.

Creed, Barbara. "Phallic Panic: Male Hysteria and Dead Ringers." *Screen* 31.2 (1990): 125–46.

Cronenberg, David. "Backtalk . . . with David Cronenberg." With Robert Hookey. *Motion* 6.4–5 (1974): 16.

_____. "David Cronenberg on Rabid." With Lee Rolfe. *Cinefantastique* 6.3 (1977): 26–27.

_____. "David Cronenberg: The Rolling Stone Interview." With David Breskin. *Rolling Stone* 6 Feb. 1992: 66+.

_____. "David Cronenberg: Sex . . . Porn . . . Censorship . . . Art . . . Politics . . . and Other Terms." With Susan Ayscough. *Cinema Canada* Dec. 1983: 15–18.

_____. "Film Making in Canada." *Film* 58 (1970): 27–28.

_____. "The Interview." With William Beard and Piers Handling. Handling 159–98.

_____. Interviews with Chris Rodley et al. Rodley.

_____. "The Night Attila Met the Anti-Christ, She Was Shocked and He Was Outraged." *Globe and Mail* [Toronto] 14 May 1977: 6.

Czarnecki, Mark. "A Vivid Obsession with Sex and Death." *Maclean's* 14 Feb. 1983: 61–63.

Delaney, Marshall [Robert Fulford]. "You Should Know How Bad This Film Is. After All, You Paid for It." Rev. of *The Parasite Murders* [*Shivers*]. *Saturday Night* Sept. 1975: 83–85.

Dompierre, Louise. *Prent/Cronenberg: Crimes against Nature*. Toronto: The Power Plant, 1987.

Dowler, Andrew. "The Brood." Rev. of *The Brood*. *Cinema Canada* Sept. 1979: 33–34.

Drew, Wayne, ed. *Dossier 21: David Cronenberg*. London: British Film Institute, 1984.

D[zeguze]., K[aspars]. "Happy Film Images and Money to Boot." *Globe and Mail* [Toronto] 18 Oct. 1969: 4.

Edwards, Natalie. "David Cronenberg's The Parasite Murders." Rev. of *The Parasite Murders*. *Cinema Canada* Oct. 1975: 44–45.

Feldman, Seth, ed. *Take Two*. Toronto: Irwin, 1984.

Feldman, Seth, and Joyce Nelson, eds. *Canadian Film Reader*. Take One Film Book Series 5. Toronto: Martin; Montreal: Take One, 1977.

Fletcher, John, and Andrew Benjamin, eds. *Abjection, Melancholia and Love: The Work of Julia Kristeva*. Warwick Studies in Philosophy and Literature. London: Routledge, 1990.

Francis, Diane. "Fun and Games on the Terror Set." *Maclean's* 9 July 1979: 4.

Fraser, Matthew. "Ontario Unreels Its Charms." *Globe and Mail* [Toronto] 20 Nov. 1990: C1.

Fulford, Robert. *Marshall Delaney at the Movies*. Take One Film Book Series 3. Toronto: Martin; Montreal: Take One, 1974.

Gleiberman, Owen. "Double Meanings." *American Film* Oct. 1988: 39–41, 43.

Govier, Katherine. "Middle-Class Shivers." *Toronto Life* July 1979: 50+.

Groen, Rick. "Of Bugs and Blobs and Duelling Dualities." *Globe and Mail* [Toronto] 11 Jan. 1992: C7.

Grunberg, Serge. *David Cronenberg*. Paris: Editions de l'étoile; Cahiers du cinéma, 1992.

Handling, Piers, ed. *The Shape of Rage: The Films of David Cronenberg*. Toronto: Academy of Canadian Cinema; General, 1983.

Harcourt, Peter. Introduction. Feldman and Nelson 370–76.

Harkness, John. "David Cronenberg's 'Scanners.' " Rev. of *Scanners*. *Cinema Canada* Mar. 1981: 34–36.

———. "Naked Lunch Suits Cronenberg's Taste." *Now* [Toronto] 9–15 Jan. 1992: 39.

Hoberman, J. "Tech It or Leave It." Rev. of *Videodrome*, dir. David Cronenberg; *In the King of Prussia*, dir. Emile de Antonio; *Petria's Wreath*, dir. Srdjan Karanović; and *Twilight Time*, dir. Goran Paskaljević. *Village Voice* [New York] 15 Feb. 1983: 50.

Hofsess, John. "Fear and Loathing to Order: How Shlockmeister David Cronenberg Served Up His Latest Smorgasbord of Outrages." *Canadian* 26 Feb. 1977: 14–17.

Irving, Joan. "Rabid." Rev. of *Rabid*. *Cinema Canada* Apr.–May 1977: 57–58.

Jaehne, Karen. "Double Trouble." *Film Comment* 24.5 (1988): 20+.

James, Noah. "The Horrifying David Cronenberg." *Maclean's* 9 July 1979: 4–7.

Johnson, Brian D. "A Fatal Obsession." *Maclean's* 19 Sept. 1988: 50–53.

Jones, Martha J. "Cronenberg on Wheels." *Cinema Canada* Sept.–Oct. 1978: 17–19.

Knelman, Martin. *This Is Where We Came In: The Career and Character of Canadian Film.* Toronto: McClelland, 1977.

Kristeva, Julia. *Soleil noir: Dépression et mélancolie.* Paris: Gallimard, 1987.

Kroll, Jack. "The Beauty of Horror." *Newsweek* 9 Mar. 1981: 73, 77.

[Lanken, Dane]. "The Parasite Murders Is Horrible." *Gazette* [Montreal] 11 Oct. 1975: 19.

Lanken, Dane. "Writer-Director Cronenberg Protests the Maniac Tag." *Gazette* [Montreal] 11 Oct. 1975: 19.

Link, André. "Delaney's Dreary Denegration [sic]." *Cinema Canada* Oct. 1975: 24.

Loorson, Charles. "No Guts, No Glory." *Première* Oct. 1988: 58–62.

Lucas, Tim. "The Image as Virus: The Filming of Videodrome." Handling 149–58.

MacInnis, Craig. "David Cronenberg: Naked Genius." *Toronto Star* 11 Jan. 1992: F1, F11.

MacMillan, Robert. "Shivers . . . Makes Your Flesh Creep!" *Cinema Canada* Mar. 1981: 11–15.

Martin, Bruce. "For $10,000 He's Making Canada's Most Controversial Movie." *Toronto Star* 13 Sept. 1969: 29.

Martin, Robert. "A Canadian Movie Wins at Box Office with a Bloody Tale of Wormy Parasites." *Globe and Mail* [Toronto] 29 June 1976: 29.

McGregor, Gaile. "Grounding the Countertext: David Cronenberg and the Ethnospecificity of Horror." *Canadian Journal of Film Studies* 2.1 (1992): 43–62.

McKinnon, John P. "Videodrome: Insidious Effects of High Tech." *Cinema Canada* Feb. 1982: 32.

Medjuck, Joe. "Stereo." Rev. of *Stereo. Take One* Jan.–Feb. 1969: 22.

Milne, Tom. "The Brood." Rev. of *The Brood. Monthly Film Bulletin* Mar. 1980: 44–45.

Morris, Peter. *The Film Companion: A Comprehensive Guide to More Than 650 Canadian Films and Filmmakers.* Toronto: Irwin, 1984.

Nerval, Gérard de. "El Desdichado." *Oeuvres.* Ed. A. Beguin and J. Richer. Paris: Pléiade, 1960.

Odier, Daniel. *The Job: Interviews with William S. Burroughs*. Rev. and enl. ed. New York: Grove, 1974.

O'Toole, Lawrence. "The Cult of Horror." Rev. of *The Brood*. *Maclean's* 16 July 1979: 46+.

____. "A Thinking Man's Nightmare." Rev. of *Videodrome*. *Maclean's* 14 Feb. 1983: 63.

Peredo, Sandra. "The Dark Mind of David Cronenberg." *Today* 28 Feb. 1981: 14–16.

Porter, John. "Artists Discovering Film/Post-War Toronto." *Vanguard* [June–Aug.] 1984: 24–26.

____. "Consolidating Film Activity/Toronto in the 60's." *Vanguard* Nov. 1984: 26–29.

Portman, Jamie. " 'Shivers' Generates Industry Shock Waves." *Citizen* [Ottawa] 18 Mar. 1976: 74.

Pringle, Douglas. "New Film in Toronto." *Artscanada* 142–43 (1970): 50–54.

Rayns, Tony. "Crimes of the Future." Rev. of *Crimes of the Future*. *Monthly Film Bulletin* Nov. 1971: 217.

____. "Stereo." Rev. of *Stereo*. *Monthly Film Bulletin* Oct. 1971: 204.

Rickey, Carrie. "Make Mine Cronenberg." *Village Voice* [New York] 1 Feb. 1983: 62, 64–65.

Rodley, Chris, ed. *Cronenberg on Cronenberg*. London: Faber, 1992.

Salem, Rob. "Let's Do Lunch Has New Meaning on Cronenberg Set." *Toronto Star* 11 Jan. 1992: F2.

Sammon, Paul M. "David Cronenberg: Canada's One-Man Horror Industry Shakes Off the Stigma of Being a 'Schlock' Director." *Cinefantastique* 10.4 (1981): 21–26, 29–34.

Sarris, Andrew. Rev. of *The Fly*. *Village Voice* [New York] 19 Aug. 1986: 47.

Scott, Jay. "Director Gets to the Heart of Horror Genre." *Globe and Mail* [Toronto] 16 Aug. 1986: C2.

____. "From Cronenberg's Kitchen, an Exotic, Steaming Lunch." Rev. of *Naked Lunch*. *Globe and Mail* [Toronto] 10 Jan. 1992: C1.

____. "A Horrifying Look at Humanity." Rev. of *The Fly*. *Globe and Mail* [Toronto] 15 Aug. 1986: A12.

Skerl, Jennie. *William S. Burroughs*. Twayne's United States Authors Series. Boston: Twayne, 1985.

Snider, Norman. "Just Two Innocent Canadian Boys in Wicked

Hollywood." *Saturday Night* July 1974: 17–22.

Stanbrook, Alan. "Cronenberg's Creative Cancers." *Sight and Sound* 58.1 (1989–90): 54–56.

Sutton, Martin. "Schlock! Horror! The Films of David Cronenberg." *Films and Filming* Oct. 1982: 15–21.

Taylor, Paul. "Scanners." Rev. of *Scanners*. *Monthly Film Bulletin* Apr. 1981: 78.

———. "Videodrome." Rev. of *Videodrome*. *Monthly Film Bulletin* Nov. 1983: 310.

Testa, Bart. "No Thrills or Chills." Rev. of *Scanners*. *Maclean's* 2 Feb. 1981: 51.

Yacowar, Maurice. "You Shiver Because It's Good." *Cinema Canada* Feb. 1977: 54–55.